Controlling airborne contaminants at work

A guide to local exhaust ventilation (LEV)

HSE Books

© Crown copyright 2008

First published 2008

ISBN 978 0 7176 6298 2

All rights reserved. No part of this publication may be reproduced, stored in a retrieval system, or transmitted in any form or by any means (electronic, mechanical, photocopying, recording or otherwise) without the prior written permission of the copyright owner.

Applications for reproduction should be made in writing to: The Office of Public Sector Information, Information Policy Team, Kew, Richmond, Surrey TW9 4DU or e-mail: licensing@opsi.gov.uk

This guidance is issued by the Health and Safety Executive. Following the guidance is not compulsory and you are free to take other action. But if you do follow the guidance you will normally be doing enough to comply with the law. Health and safety inspectors seek to secure compliance with the law and may refer to this guidance as illustrating good practice.

Contents

Chapter 1 About this book *1*

Chapter 2 Introduction to LEV, roles and responsibilities *2*

Chapter 3 Properties of airborne contaminants *6*

Chapter 4 Processes and sources *9*

Chapter 5 Preparing a specification and quotation *14*

Chapter 6 Hood design and application *18*

Chapter 7 Designing the rest of the system *37*

Chapter 8 Installing and commissioning *51*

Chapter 9 User manual and logbook *57*

Chapter 10 Thorough examination and test *60*

Appendix 1 Legal requirements *65*

Appendix 2 Selecting a 'control benchmark' and 'control requirement' *67*

References *69*

Further reading *71*

Useful contacts *72*

Glossary *73*

1 About this book

Introduction

1 Thousands of British workers contract occupational asthma and other lung diseases each year. Many people die or are permanently disabled by these conditions and are unable to work. People develop these diseases because they breathe in too much dust, fume or other airborne contaminants at work, often because control measures do not work well enough. Most industries are affected, including woodworking, welding, paint-spraying, stonemasonry, engineering and foundry work.

2 This book describes how to control gas, vapour, dust, fume and mist in workplace air using local exhaust ventilation (LEV) – extracting the clouds of contaminant before people breathe them in. It describes the principles and good practice of design, installation, commissioning, and testing of cost-effective 'ventilation controls'.

Who is this book aimed at?

3 This guidance is written for the suppliers of LEV goods and services. It will also be helpful for employers and managers in medium-sized businesses and trade union and employee safety representatives. All these people need to work together to provide effective LEV so that workers are not breathing in dangerous substances. Different chapters will be more appropriate for different audiences.

4 Employers are often unaware that their workers are being overexposed to these substances or that existing controls may be inadequate. The problems include:

- sources of exposure are missed;
- employers (and suppliers) are over-optimistic about the effectiveness of the controls;
- existing controls have deteriorated;
- the controls are not used correctly.

5 Suppliers need to help employers by:

- warning them if LEV is not the right control option;
- providing LEV that is fit for purpose, is shown to work and continues to work;
- questioning whether existing controls are working well enough.

6 Employers need a systematic and critical approach to controls, working with designers and suppliers, to avoid expensive mistakes and control exposure effectively.

What does this book include?

7 This book replaces HSG37 *An introduction to local exhaust ventilation* and HSG54 *Maintenance, examination and testing of local exhaust ventilation*. It includes information on:

- LEV and other ventilation as part of the measures needed to control exposure;
- the roles and legal responsibilities of suppliers, employers and service providers, such as those who install, commission, maintain and test LEV;
- the levels of competence people need;
- principles and good practice for design and/or supply of effective LEV, including matching the LEV to the process and the source;
- hood classification – enclosing, receiving and capturing;
- installation and commissioning;
- having a user manual and a logbook with every LEV system;
- information that the supplier should provide on checking and maintenance;
- a description of thorough examinations and tests, including red-labelling hoods with serious defects.

8 There is also a glossary of useful terms, 'References' and 'Further reading' sections and a 'Useful contacts' section.

9 This book does not cover specialised topics such as biological agents; radioactive substances; pharmaceutical containment; confined spaces and air blowers; refuges (clean rooms in contaminated environments); or cleaning systems. However, the principles of LEV design often apply in such fields.

2 Introduction to LEV, roles and responsibilities

Key points

- The employer (the LEV owner) must ensure controls are adequate.
- Everyone in the LEV supply chain must be competent.

What is local exhaust ventilation (LEV)?

10 LEV is an engineering control system to reduce exposures to airborne contaminants such as dust, mist, fume, vapour or gas in a workplace. Most systems, but not all, have the following:

Hood: This is where the contaminant cloud enters the LEV.

Ducting: This conducts air and the contaminant from the hood to the discharge point.

Air cleaner or arrestor: This filters or cleans the extracted air. Not all systems need air cleaning.

Air mover: The 'engine' that powers the extraction system, usually a fan.

Discharge: This releases the extracted air to a safe place.

11 It is vital to identify all components that may be part of the LEV system, for example:

- parts of equipment such as the machine casing or guards if they have extraction to control emissions;
- flues from hot processes, eg furnaces or ovens;
- systems to replace extracted air (make-up air), particularly where large ventilated booths extract large volumes of air from the workroom.

Roles and responsibilities

12 This book describes the principles of LEV design and application and this chapter describes the knowledge, capability and experience ('competence') required for each field of LEV practice (see Figure 2).

Employers

13 The employer is the 'system owner' and is the client for a new or redesigned LEV system. Employees, as process operators or 'LEV users', also have a vital role to play in using properly any LEV provided, checking it is effective, and reporting any faults.

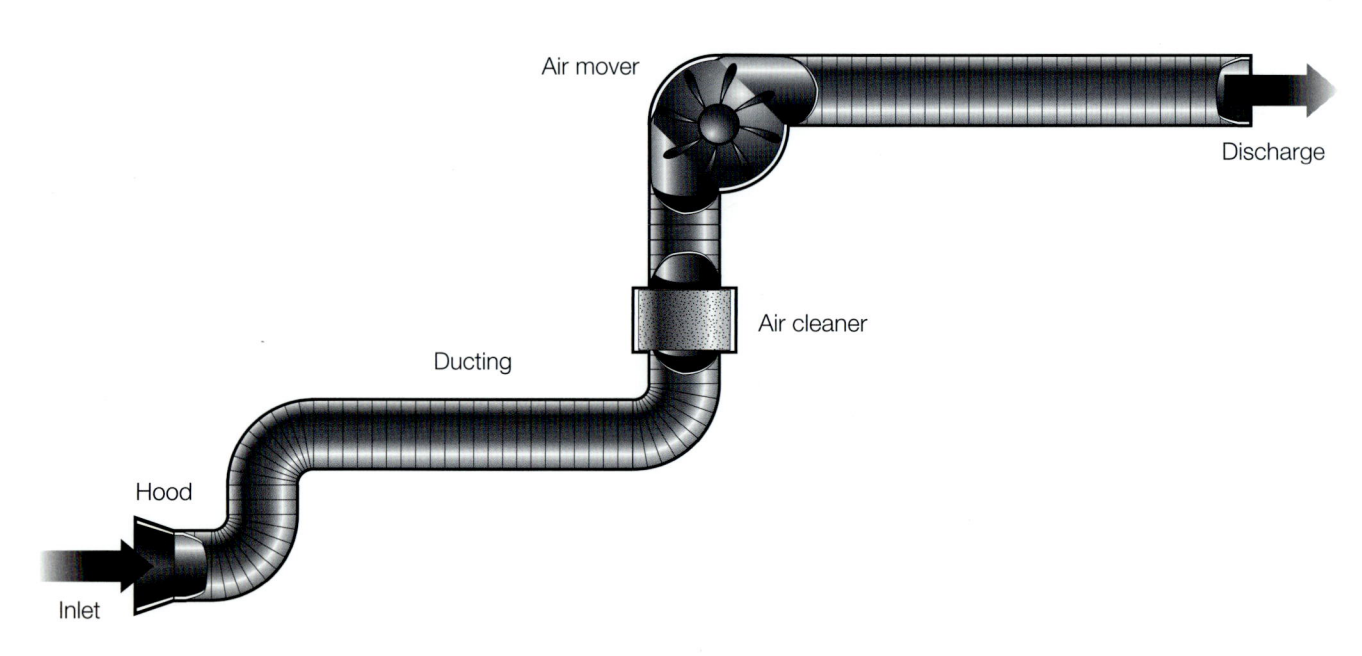

Figure 1 Common elements of a simple LEV system

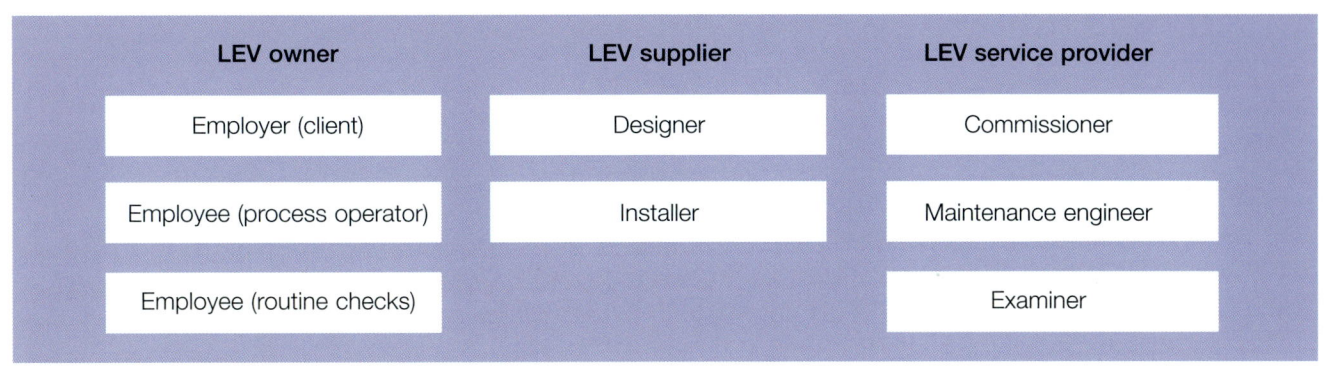

LEV owner	LEV supplier	LEV service provider
Employer (client)	Designer	Commissioner
Employee (process operator)	Installer	Maintenance engineer
Employee (routine checks)		Examiner

Figure 2 Who's who in LEV supply and ownership

What employers need to do before applying LEV

14 The employer should not apply LEV before considering other control options and using them where appropriate (see HSE leaflets INDG136[1] and INDG408[2]). In some circumstances, LEV may not be a practicable control as there may be many sources or extensive contaminant clouds that are too large for LEV alone to control. The other control options are:

- eliminate the source;
- substitute the material being used by something safer;
- reduce the size of the source;
- modify the process to reduce the frequency or duration of emission;
- reduce the number of employees involved with a process;
- apply simple controls, eg fitting lids to equipment.

What employers need to know when LEV is appropriate

- The key properties of airborne contaminants.
- How gases, vapours, dusts and mists arise.
- How contaminant clouds move with the surrounding air.
- The processes in the workplace which may be sources of airborne contaminants.
- The needs of the operators working near those sources.
- How much control will be required.
- How to prepare a specification for the LEV designer.
- What to tell the LEV supplier.

15 Employers also need to be aware of:

- the general principles of hood design and application;
- the need for airflow indicators and other instrumentation;
- capture zones, working zones and breathing zones;
- the general principles of ductwork, air movers and air cleaners and how they interact;
- the principles of how to discharge contaminated air safely and replace it with clean air;
- the process of commissioning the LEV system, including installation, performance checks, control effectiveness and reporting;
- the need for a user manual and logbook;
- the requirement for thorough examination and test of LEV.

16 The employer may use in-house staff to provide 'LEV services' if they are competent.

LEV routine checks by employees

17 The people who carry out routine checks of the LEV system are usually employees or supervisors, but may be service providers.

What employees need to know to carry out routine checks

- The parts of an LEV system and their function.
- How to recognise a damaged part from a visual inspection.
- The purpose of, and how to use, the measuring and assessment instruments and techniques.
- How to check that the LEV system is delivering its design performance and is effectively controlling emissions and exposure.

LEV suppliers and designers

18 LEV suppliers provide goods (an LEV system) and may then act as a service provider. Designers are responsible for interpreting the requirements of the employer and providing an effective LEV system which is capable of delivering the required control.

What suppliers and designers need to know

- Their role and legal responsibilities.
- How to liaise effectively with the employer and installer.
- The principles of LEV hood design.
- How to apply hood design to the processes and sources requiring control.
- How to design LEV for ease and safety of checking and maintenance.
- The specifications for airflow, duct, filter, air mover, air cleaner, discharge, instrumentation and alarms.
- The specification for in-use performance checks.
- How to prepare an LEV user manual with schedules for maintenance and statutory thorough examination and test.
- How to prepare a logbook for the system, with schedules for checks and when to replace parts.

LEV installers

19 LEV installers work with commissioners to ensure the equipment supplied provides adequate control of the contaminant. The installer may be the design company, a service provider, or even the employer (if competent).

What installers need to know

- How to install LEV systems safely.
- The basic principles of LEV hood design and proper application.
- How to install according to the specified design.
- How to modify the LEV system design, if necessary, to deliver its intended performance.
- How to liaise effectively with the designer and employer.

LEV service providers

20 Service providers offer services such as installation, commissioning, maintenance and thorough examination and tests.

LEV commissioners

21 LEV commissioners work with installers to ensure the equipment supplied provides adequate control of the contaminant.

What commissioners need to know

- Their role and legal responsibilities.
- How to liaise and communicate with the employer and employees.
- How to check that the LEV system is delivering its design performance.
- How to specify and describe the performance of the LEV system.
- How to check that exposure is effectively controlled and the LEV system is performing as planned.
- What to include in the LEV commissioning report as an adequate benchmark to compare future performance.

LEV maintenance and repair engineers

22 LEV maintenance and repair engineers are usually service providers, but sometimes an employee can carry out the work.

What maintenance and repair engineers need to know

- How to recognise and assess hazards.
- How to follow safe systems of work.
- To warn operators that maintenance is under way.
- How to minimise the spread of contamination.
- How to decontaminate themselves and areas safely.
- How to use personal protective equipment correctly, when required.
- How to use respiratory protective equipment (RPE) for access inside filter housings and ducting.
- Where smoke tracers could trigger alarms or fire alarms.
- When a dust lamp could distract other workers.

LEV examiners – statutory thorough examination and test

23 LEV examiners are usually service providers, responsible for carrying out the thorough examination and test.

What examiners need to know

- The parts of an LEV system and their function.
- The legal requirements for the thorough examination and testing of LEV systems.
- How to recognise a damaged part from a visual inspection.
- The purpose of, and how to use, the measuring and assessment instruments and techniques.
- The most suitable instrument to test the performance of each part of the LEV system.
- The standard to which each part of the LEV system should perform.
- How to recognise when a part of the LEV is performing unsatisfactorily, based on the measurements taken and assessment methods used.
- How to assess whether the LEV is effectively reducing airborne contaminant emission and operator exposure.
- How to collate and record information in a clear, concise and useable way.
- How to work safely with the LEV plant and the hazards associated with it.

Legal responsibilities

24 People who supply, own and use LEV have legal duties:

- The employer of the people being protected by the LEV has legal responsibilities under the Health and Safety at Work etc Act 1974, the Control of Substances Hazardous to Health Regulations (COSHH) 2002 (as amended)[3] and the Management of Health and Safety at Work Regulations 1999 (MHSWR).[4] There are also special provisions for employers in Safety Data Sheets under REACH[5] (see paragraphs 82-86).
- LEV suppliers have legal responsibilities under the Health and Safety at Work etc Act 1974; the Supply of Machinery (Safety) Regulations 1992 (as amended) (SMSR),[6] including 'essential health and safety requirements'.
- Service providers have legal responsibilities under the Health and Safety at Work etc Act 1974 and the Construction (Design and Management) Regulations 2007.[7]

25 For more about legal responsibilities, see Appendix 1.

Competence

26 Another legal requirement under MHSWR and COSHH is 'competence'. This means people having the appropriate knowledge, capabilities and experience to carry out the job they are employed to do. Competence requirements apply to whoever:

- designs or selects control measures;
- checks, tests and maintains control measures;
- supplies goods and services to employers for health and safety purposes.

27 The requirement for competence for suppliers of goods and services means that the extent and depth of their knowledge and capability must be sufficient to assess and solve the problems they are likely to meet.

28 The more complex a control scenario is and the more serious the results of failure, the greater the degree of competence required. For example:

- Simple, routine, specified work requires basic knowledge and training.
- Complex work requires recognised and appropriate qualifications, much greater knowledge and demonstrated success at applying this knowledge to a variety of problems.

29 Many trades recognise levels of competence based on qualifications and tests of capability, as well as experience of successful problem-solving over a number of years. See Appendix 1 for more information on becoming 'competent'.

30 The employer decides who to employ or consult, and needs to be an 'intelligent customer' to get the best result. HSE has produced simple guidance to help the employer choose a supplier when buying LEV (see HSE leaflet INDG408[2]). Suppliers need to prepare their information to respond to this approach.

Training courses

31 Those wishing to improve their LEV knowledge and skills should consider attending a suitable training course providing qualifications such as:

- BOHS P601 Proficiency Module: Initial appraisal and thorough examination and testing of local exhaust ventilation systems;
- BOHS P602 Proficiency Module: Basic design principles of local exhaust ventilation systems;
- BOHS Cert.OH: Certificate of Operational Competence in Occupational Hygiene;
- BOHS Dip.OH: Diploma of Professional Competence in Occupational Hygiene.

32 See www.bohs.org for more information.

3 Properties of airborne contaminants

Key points

- Gases, vapours, dusts, fumes and mists arise differently.
- Once in air, all contaminant clouds move with the air that surrounds them.

33 This chapter descibes the behaviour of airborne contaminants and removes some common misconceptions.

Airborne contaminants

34 Air contaminants are particles, gases or vapours and combinations of these. 'Particles' include dusts, fumes, mists and fibres. Table 1 shows some of the basic characteristics of airborne contaminants.

Table 1 Some properties of airborne contaminants

Name	Description and size	Visibility	Examples
Dust	Solid particles – can be supplied, eg powder-handling, or process generated, eg crushing and grinding. Inhalable particle size 0.01 to 100 μm. Respirable particle size below 10 μm.	In diffuse light: ■ Inhalable dust clouds are partially visible. ■ Respirable dust clouds are practically invisible at concentrations up to tens of mg/m^3.	Grain dust, wood dust, silica flour.
Fume	Vapourised solid that has condensed. Particle size 0.001 μm to 1 μm.	Fume clouds tend to be dense. They are partially visible. Fume and smoke are generally more visible than equivalent concentrations of dust.	Rubber fume, solder fume, welding fume.
Mist	Liquid particles – process generated, eg by spraying. Particle size ranges 0.01 to 100 μm but the size distribution may change as volatile liquids evaporate.	As for dust.	Electroplating, paint sprays, steam.
Fibres	Solid particles – the length is several times the diameter. Particle size – as for dust.	As for dust.	Asbestos, glass fibre.
Vapour	The gaseous phase of a liquid or solid at room temperature. Behaves as a gas.	Usually invisible. At very high concentrations, a vapour-laden cloud may just be visible.	Styrene, petrol, acetone, mercury, iodine.
Gas	A gas at room temperature.	Usually invisible – some coloured at high concentrations.	Chlorine, carbon monoxide.

Particles

Particle size of contaminant clouds

35 The size of particles determines whether they are 'inhalable' or 'respirable':

- Particles that are small enough to be breathed in are called 'inhalable' particles. They range in size from less than 0.01 μm up to 100 μm aerodynamic diameter.
- Clouds of inhalable particles contain smaller 'respirable' particles that can penetrate deeply into the lungs. They have an upper size limit of about 10 μm.
- Particles above 100 μm are not 'inhalable' as they are too large to be breathed in. They fall out of the air and settle on the floor and surfaces near the process.

36 There are strict definitions and standardised methods for sampling inhalable and respirable particles (see MDHS14/3[8] *General methods for sampling and gravimetric analysis of respirable and inhalable dust*).

Visibility of particle clouds

37 What you can see is not necessarily all that is there:

- When a cloud contains mainly respirable particles, it is practically invisible to the naked eye.
- When the cloud contains inhalable particles, it is partially visible.
- Mist and fume clouds are more visible than the equivalent concentration of dust.

38 Most particles in dust clouds from organic material such as wood or flour are mainly inhalable, with a minor proportion of respirable particles.

39 Most particles in dust clouds from minerals (eg stone, concrete) are mainly respirable, with a minor proportion of inhalable particles. But the larger particles make up the majority of the dust weight.

40 The full extent of an airborne cloud is rarely visible. In some cases, such as when all the particles are smaller than 'inhalable', it will be completely invisible. Tyndall illumination uses the forward scattering of light to show up the cloud (see Chapter 8). Alternatively, if smoke is released into the cloud, this will show up its shape, size, speed and direction. This information is essential for applying suitable LEV.

Movement of particles in air

41 Particles in contaminant clouds move with the air in which they are suspended. For example:

- Particles larger than 100 μm travel some distance if ejected at high speed but settle out quickly.
- Particles around 100 μm settle out of the air near the process which generated them (depending on the strength of local air movement).
- Smaller particles float and remain suspended in the air (this may be for several minutes) and move with air currents. This means that, where a process generates rapidly moving air streams (eg grinding wheels or circular saws), fine dust will be carried a long way from the source, making dust control difficult.

'Heavy dust'

42 Particle size, not density, determines how particles move in the air. However, many people think that dense materials produce 'heavy dust'. They therefore place LEV hoods at floor level. This does not work because:

- large particles, even of low-density material such as plastic dust, fall out of the air easily;
- small particles, even of high-density material such as lead dust, can float away in a contaminant cloud.

43 LEV needs to remove both suspended inhalable particles and intercept the larger particles. For some processes, eg on a woodworking saw, LEV collects and conveys both dust and chips.

Other properties of airborne particles

44 Process-generated and process-related substances (dust, fume, mist) may have abrasive or sticky properties, or be liable to condense. Some may be flammable. These properties determine the design of LEV.

Abrasive or corrosive particles

45 Some particles are more abrasive than others and some are more chemically active and may attack the LEV system components. This may severely restrict the selection of materials used to construct the LEV system (see Chapter 7).

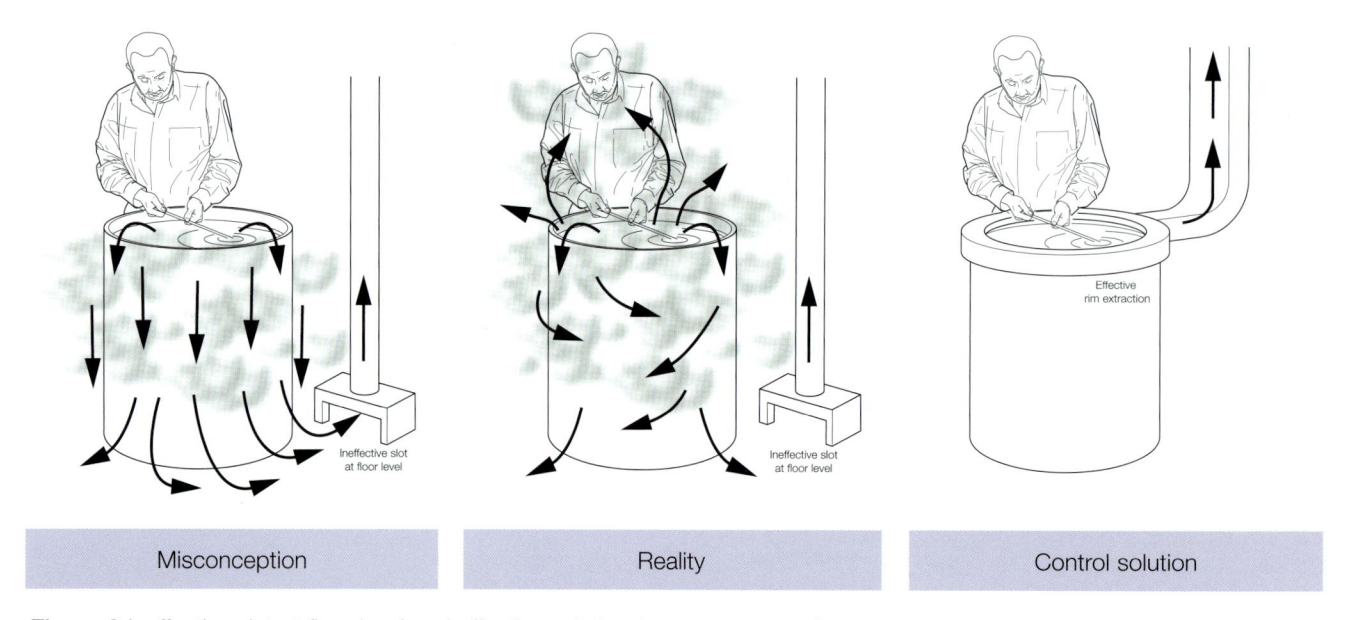

Figure 3 Ineffective slot at floor level and effective solution for vapour control

Sticky dust, mist and condensate

46 If a particulate is sticky or likely to condense, the LEV design needs to take account of this. A heavy condensate can block ducts partially or completely, and this effect is progressive rather than sudden. The design of the system must incorporate drain points for condensates, and access points to ease inspection and cleaning.

Flammable or combustible substances

47 Many organic and metal dusts are combustible and LEV systems need to reduce the chances of ignition and cope with a possible dust explosion. This book does not cover flammability issues such as zoning[9] or explosion relief.[10] Where such hazards exist, the design needs to take them into account.

Gas and vapour-air mixtures

- Vapours and gases move with the air.
- Vapours and gases are capable of penetrating deeply into the lungs.

'Heavy vapours'

48 There are few circumstances where dense vapours or gases sink. This is most commonly a risk in unoccupied and unventilated storage areas. When liquids are used in processes, their vapours do not tend to sink.

49 Safety Data Sheets may lead to comparing molecular weights, eg of hexane (86) with air (29), wrongly assuming the vapour cloud is three times as heavy. However, the concentration of hexane vapour at room temperature is not 100%, it is less than 20% with 80% air. So hexane-air vapour at room temperature is less than 1.4 times the weight of clean air. Mixing with workplace air and diffusion dilutes the hexane vapour even further. The mixture moves with the surrounding air and does not sink.

50 As with 'heavy dust', assumptions based on the 'heavy vapour' misconception mean that some systems have extract hoods placed low down on the floor. This can lead to control failures, as illustrated in Figure 3. The third illustration suggests a potential control solution.

51 LEV at floor level cannot provide adequate control for gases or vapours because:

- the difference in density between gas or vapour clouds and air is small;
- flowing vapour-air mixtures dilute with workroom air and the difference becomes even smaller;
- general air movement carries the mixture away.

52 Controls should be placed as close to the source as possible.

4 Processes and sources

Key point

- Effective application of LEV requires good understanding of the process and sources.

53 This chapter describes how airborne contaminants arise.

What are processes and sources?

54 When developing exposure control measures, 'process' means the way airborne contaminants are generated, for example in woodworking, processes would be cutting, shaping and sanding. The source is where the contaminant is generated by a process. Understanding the process means understanding the creation of 'sources'. This can suggest ways to modify the process to reduce the number or size of sources, and contaminant clouds. The effective application of LEV requires a good understanding of the process and the sources (see Figure 4).

55 Sources fall into four general types:

- buoyant, eg hot fume;
- injected into moving air, eg by a spray-gun;
- dispersed into workplace air, eg draughts; and
- directional, of which there are at least five sub-types – see Figure 5 showing processes and sources in stonemasonry.

56 It is crucial that the LEV system designer understands how the source behaves in its location at the specific workplace.

Figure 4 The source and contaminant cloud concepts for an angle grinder

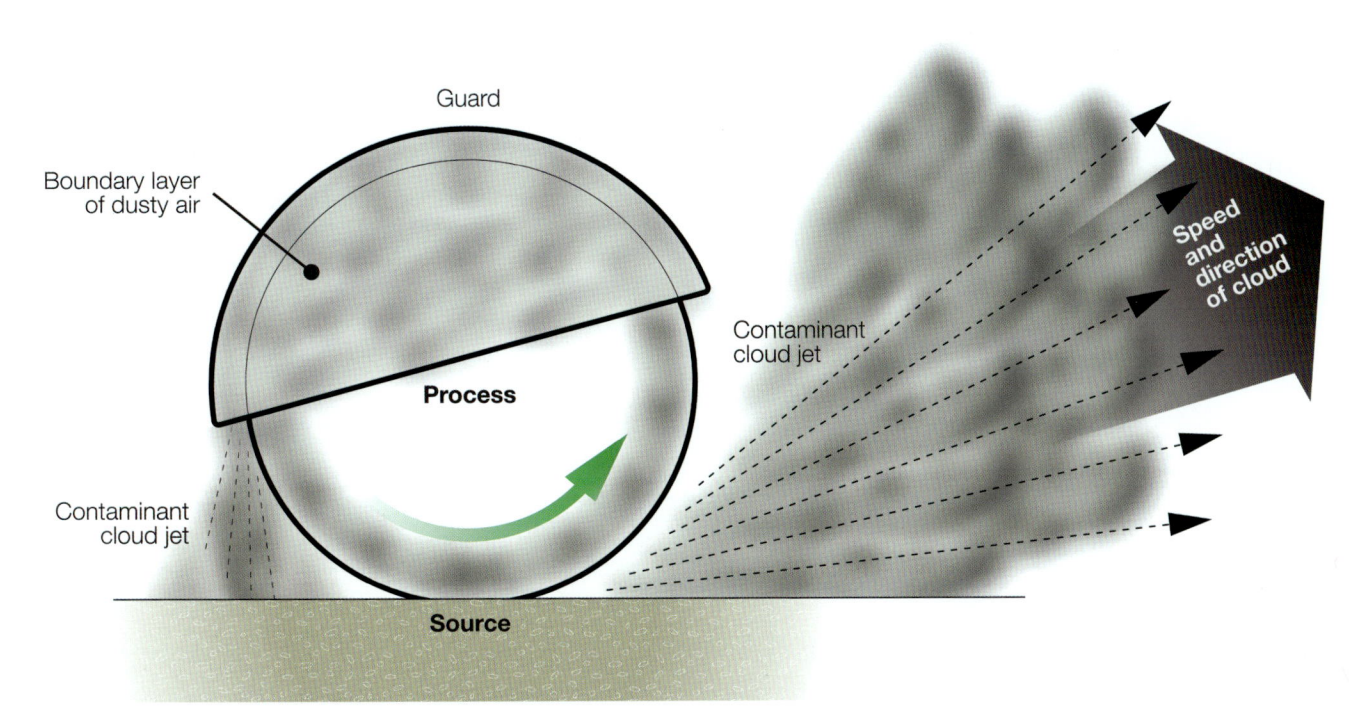

Figure 5 Processes and sources in stonemasonry

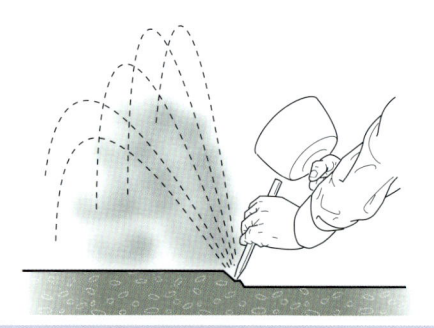

'Explosive' release

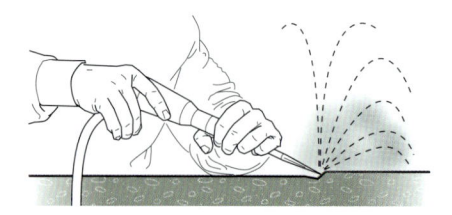

Progressive release

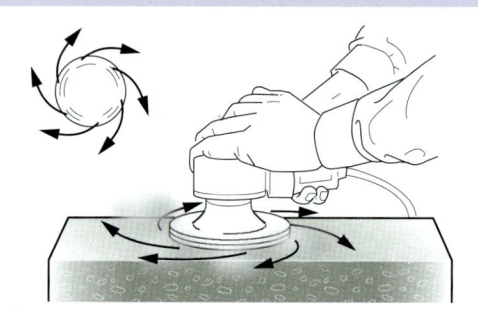

Doughnut-shaped release around rotating disc

Broad fan-shaped release from rotating disc

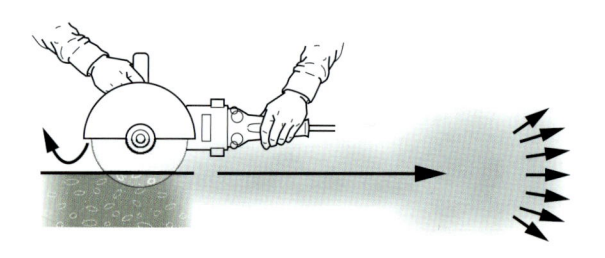

Narrow jet release from cutting trench

Source strength

57 The strength of the source is described in terms of the area from which contaminant arises, the flow of contaminant away from the source and the concentration of contaminant within the cloud. The stringency of the control requirement is determined by a combination of the:

- source strength;
- cloud volume, shape and speed and its direction of movement;
- contaminant concentration.

58 The further a contaminant moves away from its source, the larger the cloud grows through mixing and diffusion. Dilution reduces the concentration of the contaminant in the cloud. But it is always more effective to apply control close to the source of an airborne release because:

- the cloud volume is smaller, so it is easier to control;
- full interception of the whole cloud is more likely;
- the contaminant is less likely to enter the operator's breathing zone.

59 One process can create several sources at different stages. For example, Figure 4 shows two of the contaminant clouds arising from a grinding process: a third cloud would arise from the boundary layer; a fourth from the re-suspension of settled dust; and a fifth from dust deposited on protective clothing. Good control requires examining all of the activities and **all** of the sources of release from the process in question.

60 Figure 6 shows an LEV system to control dust from sack emptying. But the sack disposal is uncontrolled: this source is commonly missed. Figure 7 shows a sack-tipping hood to control dust when disposing of emptied sacks.

Figure 6 An LEV system to control dust from sack emptying, but uncontrolled sack disposal

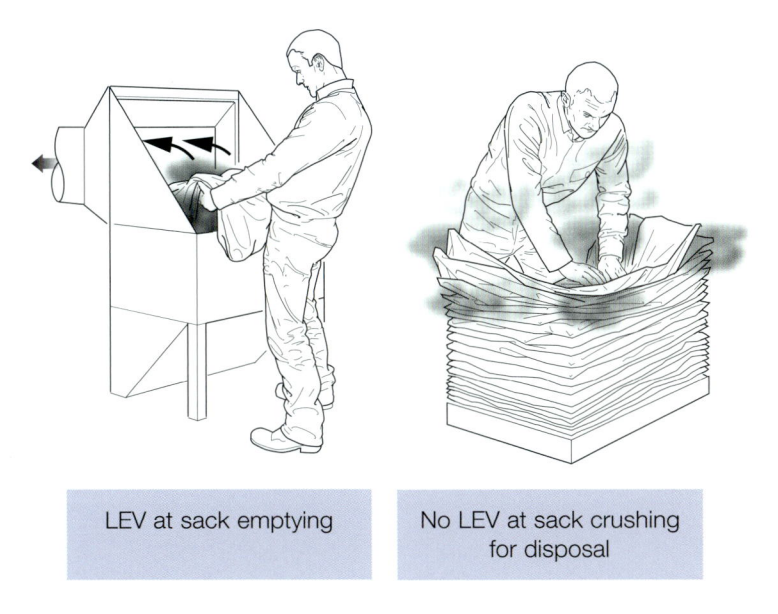

LEV at sack emptying

No LEV at sack crushing for disposal

Figure 7 A sack-tipping hood to control dust from disposal of emptied sacks

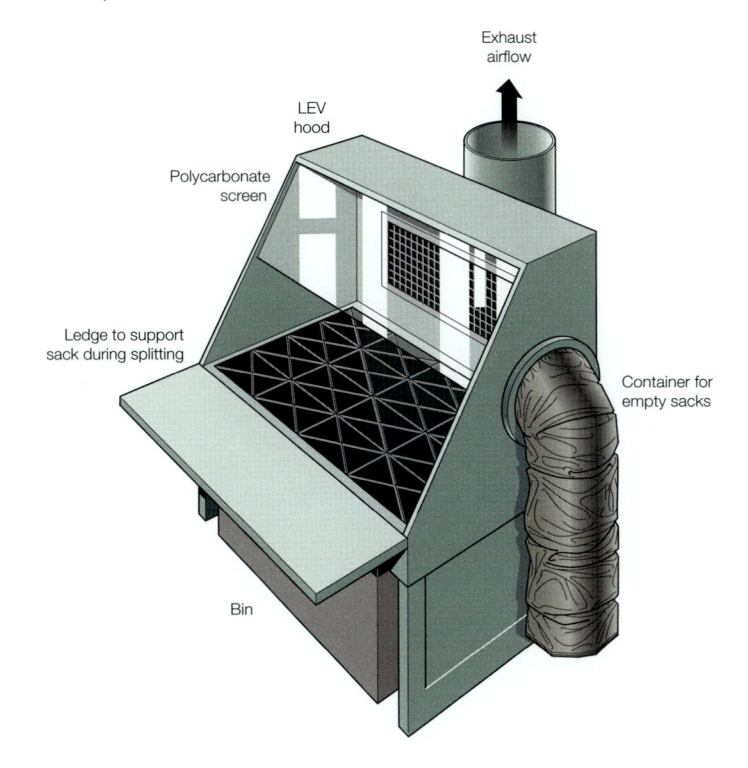

Table 2 Common processes and sources (see www.hse.gov.uk/lev for examples)

Process	Examples	Creation mechanism(s) and source description	Form	Possible controls
Rotating tools and parts	Orbital, belt and disc sanders. Disc cutters. Circular saws and routers. Lathes. Drills. Abrasive wheels.	Rotating motion creates a fan effect. The source created can be a jet (eg angle grinder with guard) or a doughnut-shaped cloud (eg disc sander).	Dust, mist.	■ Enclose. ■ Strip off the 'boundary layer' of dust-laden air moving with the rotating disc. ■ Fit a receiving hood to the guard. ■ Use LVHV (low volume high velocity extraction). Other controls, eg: ■ water suppression.
Hot (and cold) processes	Furnaces and casting. Soldering and brazing. Welding. Using liquid nitrogen.	Hot sources – fume rises, expands, cools and mixes with the room air. Cold sources – the contaminant sinks.	Fume, vapour, gas.	■ Enclose. ■ Receive the hot fume or cold contaminant cloud in a hood. Other controls, eg: ■ control temperatures to reduce fume.
Free-falling, solids, liquids and powders	Falling liquid, powder or solid material. Conveyor transfer of powders/solids.	Falling material induces a downward flow of air. If the material is a powder, there will be some shearing of fine particle-laden air at the edges of the stream. The entrained air and dust may 'splash'.	Dust, vapour.	■ Reduce the fall distance. ■ Enclose. ■ Seal gaps in conveyors. ■ Partially enclose transfer points.
Displacement	Liquid, powder and granular solid transfer into a container.	Materials displace their own volume of contaminated air from the container. If they have fallen from a height, the induced airflow will displace even more air from the container.	Dust, vapour.	■ Partial enclosure. ■ Reduce the fall distance. ■ Minimise the container's open area. ■ Make the container a receiving hood. Other controls, eg: ■ pump liquids through pipes extending to the bottom of the container; ■ use a vapour recovery system.
Spraying and blasting	Paint spraying. Abrasive blasting.	Compressed air pressure produces a jet that induces further air movement. The contaminant cloud is cone-shaped. A paint spray gun can emit air at more than 100 m/s, extending more than 12 m.	Mist, vapour, dust.	■ Reduce air pressure, eg HVLP (high volume low pressure) spray gun. ■ Full, room or part enclosure. Other controls, eg use: ■ water-borne abrasive; ■ abrasive shot, not mineral; ■ electrostatic methods for surface coating.

Process	Examples	Creation mechanism(s) and source description	Form	Possible controls
Fracturing solids	Rock crushing. Hardcore – concrete crushing. Splitting (eg slate making).	Brittle fracture creates 'explosive' release of a dust cloud. Material movement may then create airflow or assist the dust cloud growth.	Dust.	■ Full or partial enclosure. ■ Receiving, push-pull or capturing hood. Other controls, eg: ■ water suppression; ■ supplementary RPE often needed.
Impact and vibration	Dumping dusty sacks on a surface. Machinery vibration re-suspending settled dust.	Shock of the physical impact or vibration creates a dust cloud. Dust-contaminated clothing can also create a dust cloud. Settled dust can re-suspend in the air.	Dust	■ Partial enclosure. Other controls, eg: ■ control spillage; ■ vacuum system for cleaning; ■ minimise impact and vibration.
Compaction	Waste crushing.	Compaction creates a dust cloud. Material movement may then create airflow.	Dust.	■ Extract compactor in its own enclosure. ■ Partial enclosure.
Handling	Sorting.	Recycling waste.	Dust, mist.	■ Local air displacement.
Machining	Milling. Turning.	Cooling fluid on rotating or reciprocating movement.	Mist.	■ Full enclosure. ■ Partial enclosure. Other controls, eg: ■ cold working; ■ increase fluid flow to increase cooling.
Abrasion	Sanding. Grinding. Polishing. Fettling.	Mechanical removal of surfaces create airborne dust.	Dust.	■ Capturing hood, eg downdraught or back-draught table. ■ Partial enclosure, eg booth. ■ LVHV systems. Other controls, eg: ■ water suppression.
Sweeping	Dust and particulate matter.	Re-suspending settled dust – a dust cloud moving in the direction of brushing.	Dust.	Other controls, eg: ■ minimise dust leaks; ■ vacuum system; ■ wet cleaning.

5 Preparing a specification and quotation

Key point

- The employer and the supplier need to work together to develop successful control solutions.

61 This chapter describes the issues to cover in specification and quotation.

Exposure control measures

62 It is important to think about controlling exposure as more than just buying and installing the equipment. Effective exposure control measures consist of a mixture of control 'hardware' (engineering) and work practices (procedures for using the hardware).

Control hardware

63 This means all equipment, alerts and design features to control contaminant clouds. It often includes LEV, but may also include handling equipment, positioning jigs, temporary screens and elements with a design life. For example, the effectiveness of the joint seals of an enclosed conveyor may be important in minimising emissions and exposure.

Work practices

64 This covers everything that the employer and operators need to know and do to achieve control when using the hardware. It includes managing the system, supervising operators and regularly reviewing and maintaining control measures. For example, the joint seals of an enclosed conveyor need regular checking and replacement.

Developing the LEV specification

65 To draw up a specification, the employer needs to establish clearly where (and how) to apply LEV. That means identifying the processes and sources, and deciding upon the degree of control required.

Simple LEV systems

66 These are standard designs of LEV that are known to be effective. They are appropriate when there is no process modification necessary and the requirements are clear. Systems may even be available for supply 'off the shelf'. The employer, as client, may be competent to specify, procure, install and commission such simple LEV systems.

Complex processes

67 Complex processes often require expert design and the employer, as the client, may need to work closely with the expert. A 'client' is defined in the Construction (Design and Management) Regulations 2007[7] as anyone having construction or building work carried out as part of their business.

68 Exposure of workers depends on a range of process factors including the source strength and how near people are to it. The designer needs the facts about the process, source and contaminant requiring control. The employer is responsible for the specification and should supply these facts as the 'client'. This is likely to require joint effort with the designer. However, the supplier or designer may need to prompt the employer because employers do not procure new LEV very often.

Complex LEV systems

69 These are non-standard designs of LEV. Figure 8 illustrates the interdependent factors that lead to effective control. The employer and supplier need to consider these factors.

Employer

70 The employer should be aware of the contaminant cloud characteristics, the requirements of the work process and the operator's requirements – elements A, B and C in Figure 8. This information forms part of the specification for tender. An 'industry standard' of LEV makes the tendering process simpler – as long as the 'industry standard' is effective.

Supplier

71 The potential supplier should verify, or help the employer define, the contaminant cloud characteristics, the requirements of the work process and the operator's requirements – elements A, B and C in Figure 8. The potential supplier selects a suitable LEV hood – element D in Figure 8.

Supplier and employer together

72 The supplier and employer should work together, perhaps with consultants, as a project team to develop the contract. The objective is to ensure that between them, they cover adequately all elements – the contaminant cloud, the work process, the operator requirements and the hood requirements.

73 Failure to cover these elements can result in ineffective, unreliable, or expensive LEV, or all of these.

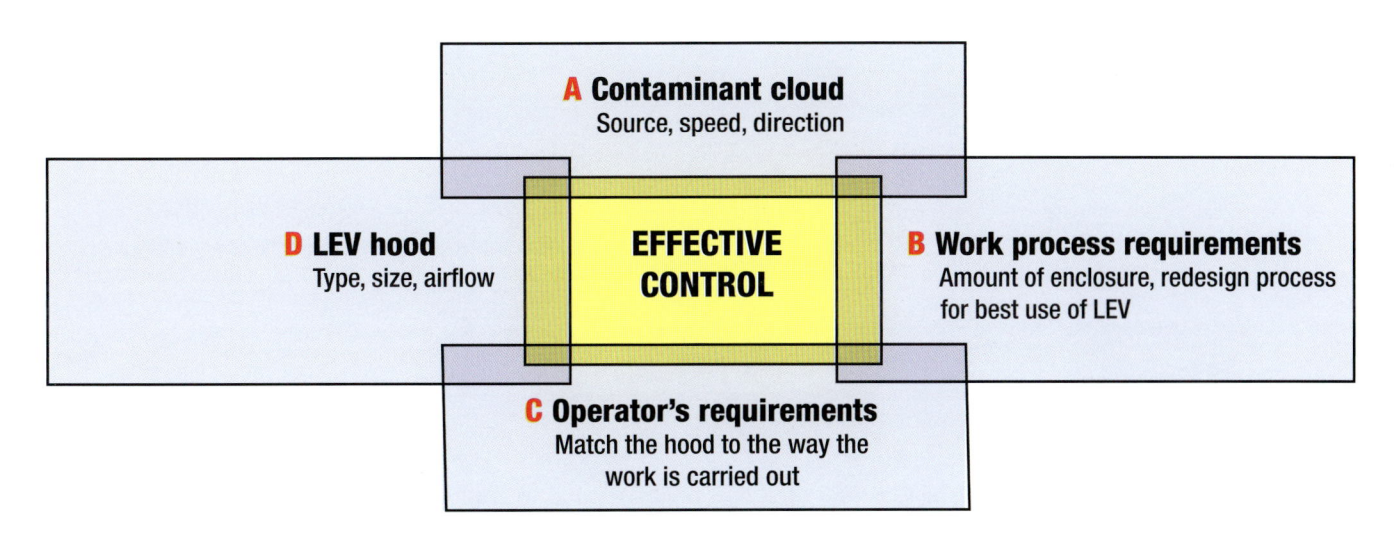

```
                    A Contaminant cloud
                    Source, speed, direction

D LEV hood              EFFECTIVE        B Work process requirements
Type, size, airflow      CONTROL         Amount of enclosure, redesign process
                                         for best use of LEV

                    C Operator's requirements
                    Match the hood to the way the
                    work is carried out
```

Figure 8 Developing effective LEV for more complex systems

Criteria for an LEV specification

74 The employer:

- should describe the process, the contaminant, its hazards, the sources to be controlled, and exposure benchmarks (see Appendix 2). The important chemical and flammable properties of substances and products appear in the Safety Data Sheet;
- may need to take advice from a competent person concerning the type of LEV to be used, its effectiveness in controlling exposures and its costs;
- should require indicators to be fitted to show that the system is working properly;
- should require the LEV to be easy to use, check, maintain and clean, taking account of other risks, eg accessibility, skin contamination, and waste removal and filter changing without spreading contamination;
- should specify that the supplier provides training in how to use, check and maintain the LEV system;
- should require that the supplier provides a user manual that describes and explains the LEV system, and how to use, check, maintain and test it, along with performance benchmarks and schedules for replacement of parts;
- should require that the supplier provides a logbook for the system to record the results of checks and maintenance.

75 It is the employer's responsibility to comply with the requirements of environmental legislation (see paragraph 227). In practice, the supplier is in a good position to advise about this.

From specification to quotation

76 The supplier's quotation is a detailed description of the proposed LEV system.

Criteria for an LEV quotation

77 The potential supplier should:

- provide technical drawings of the system;
- state the type of hood for each source, its location or position, face velocity, static pressure;
- include information on any constraints, eg the maximum number of hoods in use at any one time;
- describe the ducts – material, dimensions, transport velocity (if appropriate) and volume flow rate;
- include details of how the airflows in different branches of the LEV will be balanced;
- describe any air cleaner – specification, volume flow rate, and static pressure ranges at inlet, outlet and across the cleaner;
- describe the fan or other air mover – specification, volume flow rate, static pressure at inlet, and direction of rotation of fan;
- for systems that return air to the workplace, provide information on air cleaner efficiency and sensors;
- describe the indicators and alarms to be provided in the system;
- provide information on the installation requirements;
- provide adequate training in using, checking and maintaining the LEV system;
- provide both a user manual and a logbook.

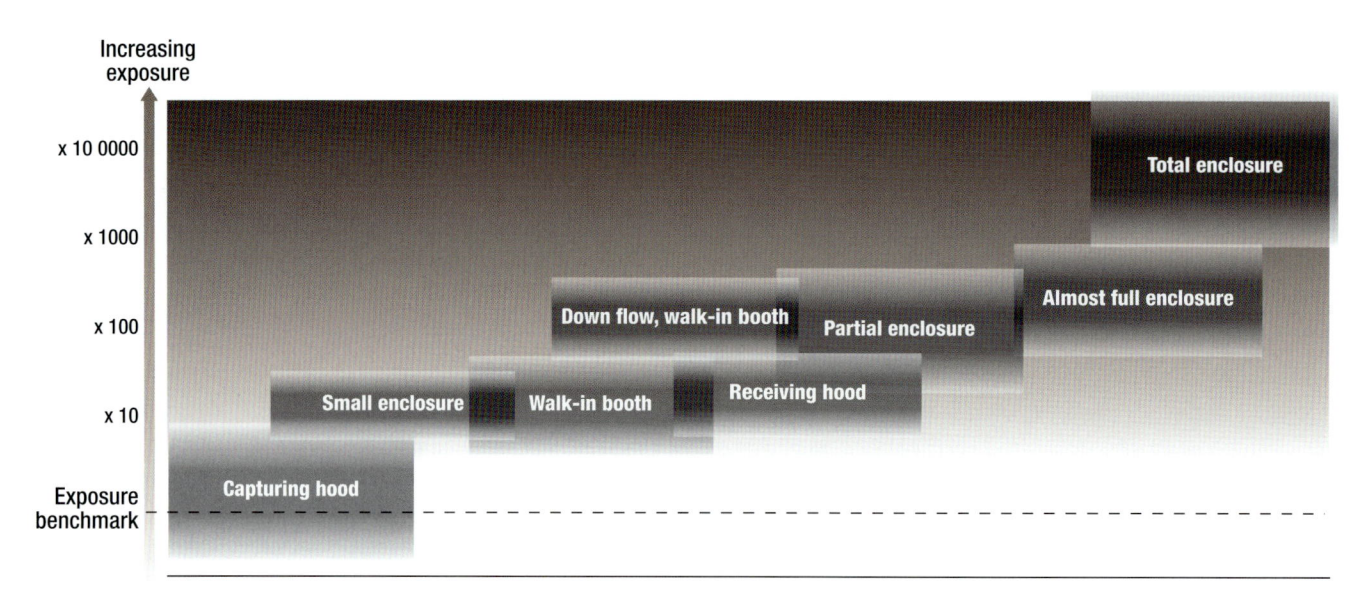

Figure 9 Effectiveness of various types of LEV

78 The designer needs to understand how effective LEV is in each specific situation. It should be capable of adequately controlling the contaminant cloud. For example, an LEV hood capable of reducing exposure 10-fold is unsuitable to control a source capable of emission at 50 times a benchmark exposure value. However, there is limited information on the effectiveness of LEV. Figure 9 proposes some indicative ranges for the effectiveness of various types of LEV.

Other issues to help produce the specification

Exposure benchmark

79 Employers need to be clear from the outset for which processes and sources the new LEV is required. They should also state a benchmark in the specification for LEV – the exposure that may result once the control is in place. This is likely to require expert advice. A suitable exposure benchmark would be a fraction of a substance's exposure limit.

80 But many substances – including substances in mixtures – do not have exposure limits. One way forward is to use a variation of 'COSHH essentials' taking account of its technical basis[11] (www.coshh-essentials.org.uk/assets/live/cetb.pdf). The scheme uses information that should be readily available on the substance or product: risk phrase (R) numbers that describe toxicity are stated in Part 15 of the Safety Data Sheet. The steps you need to take are in Appendix 2.

LEV and COSHH essentials

81 'COSHH essentials' (www.coshh-essentials.org.uk)[12] is an online system for employers in small and medium-sized businesses which helps identify the level of control required for a task. It uses substance toxicity, dustiness or volatility, quantity and time for the task. It can inform but does not constrain the decisions of LEV suppliers and designers.

REACH

82 REACH is a new European Union regulation concerning the **R**egistration, **E**valuation, **A**uthorisation and restriction of **CH**emicals. It came into force on 1 June 2007 and replaces a number of European Directives and Regulations with a single system.

83 A major part of REACH is the requirement for manufacturers or importers of substances to register them with a central European Chemicals Agency (EChA). A registration package will be supported by a standard set of data on that substance. The amount of data required is proportionate to the amount of substance manufactured or supplied. Companies that use chemicals have a duty to use them in a safe way, and information on risk management measures (RMMs), including LEV, needs to be passed down the supply chain.

84 Information exchange is a key feature of REACH. Users should be able to understand what manufacturers and importers know about the dangers involved in using chemicals and how to control these risks. However, chemical suppliers need information from the users about how they are used so that they can assess the risks. REACH provides a framework in which information can be passed both up and down supply chains.

85 REACH adopts and builds on the previous system for passing information – the Safety Data Sheet. This should accompany materials through the supply chain, providing the information users need to ensure chemicals are managed safely. Safety Data Sheets will, in time, include information on safe handling and use. There is a duty on 'downstream users' (employers) to apply the risk management measures specified in the Safety Data Sheets.

86 The HSE website (ww.hse.gov.uk/reach/index.htm) explains more about REACH.[5]

Table 3 Applying LEV: Common design issues for the supplier

Issue	Potential solution
Employer's LEV requirement not clear	Employer to look at INDG408 *Clearing the air: A simple guide to buying and using local exhaust ventilation (LEV)*.[2]
Contaminant cloud behaviour not known	Characterise the cloud strength – volume rate of release, volume, shape, speed, direction and contaminant concentration. Identify all contaminant clouds, including partly visible clouds.
Type of LEV	Follow risk management measures (REACH). Consider control approach (for example, use COSHH essentials). Use enclosing, receiving or capturing hood, or a variant of these, capable of effective control.
Design of hood, duct, air cleaner, air mover and safe discharge	See Chapters 6 and 7.
Does the quotation address all the requirements in the employer's specification?	Identify processes and sources to be controlled. Assess the required reduction of potential exposure. Include system instrumentation, including hood manometers. Include arrangements for training users. Provide a user manual and logbook for the system.

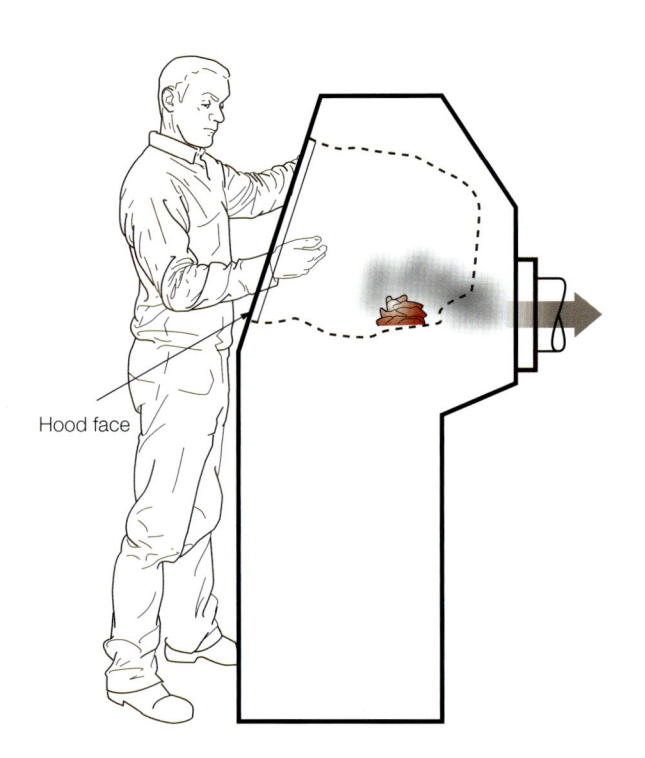

Figure 11 Enclosing hood

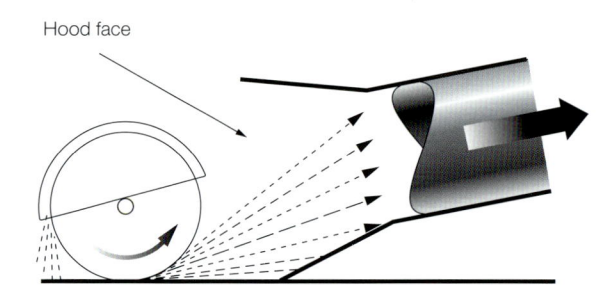

Figure 12 Receiving hood

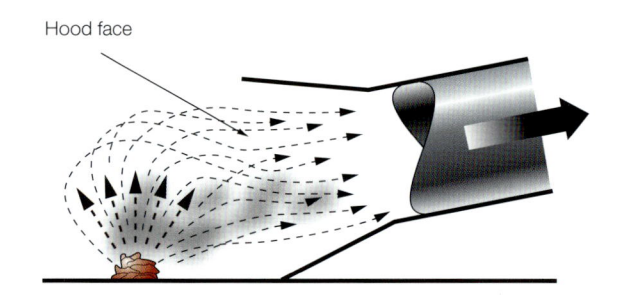

Figure 13 Capturing hood

Enclosing hood

97   Enclosures are always more effective than capturing or receiving hoods. A full enclosure is where the process is completely enclosed, eg a glove box. A room enclosure or enclosing room is where the operator and the process are enclosed, eg abrasive-blasting rooms or paint-spraying cabins. They may also be called laminar flow rooms or booths. A partial enclosure contains the process with openings for material and/or operator access, eg walk-in booths and fume cupboards.

Receiving hood

98   The process usually takes place outside the hood. The hood receives the contaminant cloud, which has a speed and direction that is usually process-generated. Hoods can be fixed or moveable. A canopy hood over a hot process is a classic receiving hood. A push-pull system is a special type of receiving hood.

Capturing hood

99   This is the most common type of LEV hood and is sometimes called a captor or capture hood. The process, source and contaminant cloud are outside the hood. A capturing hood has to generate sufficient airflow at and around the source to 'capture' and draw in the contaminant-laden air. They all work on the same principles, but can range in size from a few millimetres for on-tool extraction to metres long in large industrial processes. Hoods can be fixed or moveable. They include rim/lip extraction (slot), downdraught tables or benches and LVHV (low volume high velocity) hoods.

| Volume flow rate = 100% | Volume flow rate reduced 10-fold | Volume flow rate reduced 100-fold |

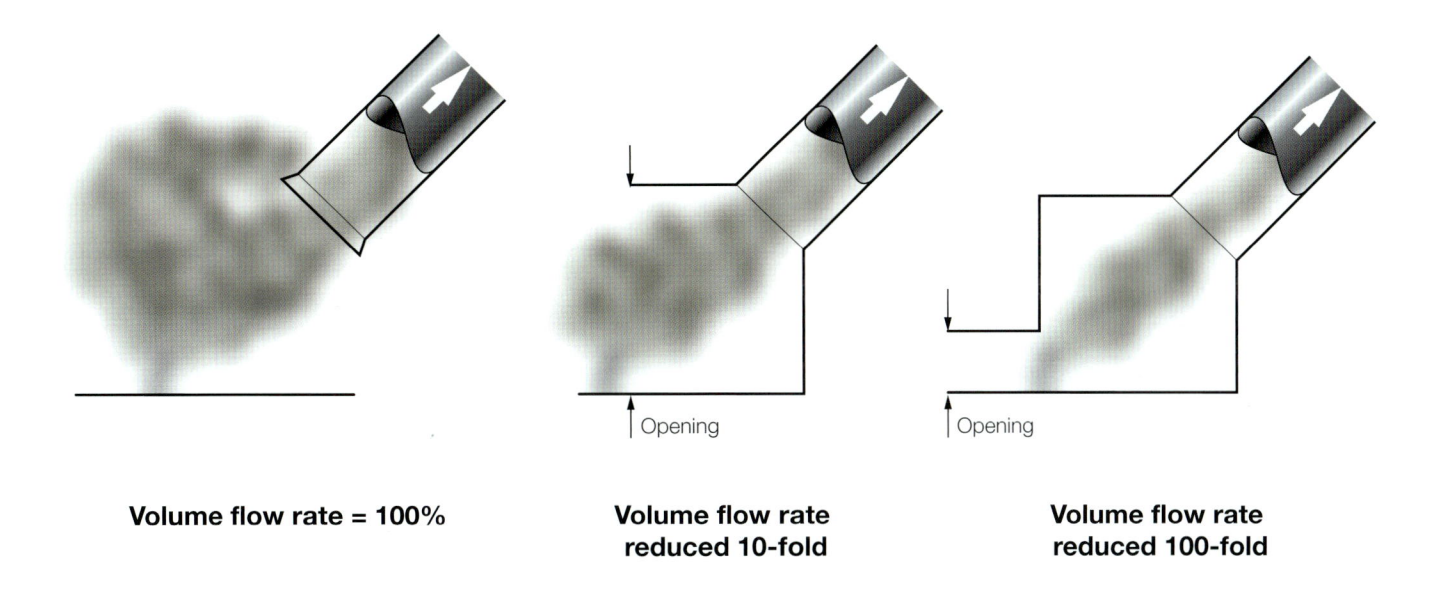

Figure 14 Maximise enclosure for effectiveness and efficiency

General principles of LEV hood design and application

100 The general principles of LEV hood design and application are:

- Maximise the enclosure of the process and source, because the greater the degree of enclosure, the more likely it is that the LEV will be effective.
- Ensure the hood is as close as possible to the process and source.
- Position the hood to take advantage of the speed and direction of the airflow from the source.
- Match the hood size to the process and contaminant cloud size.
- Separate the contaminant cloud from the worker's breathing zone as much as possible.
- Minimise eddies within the hood.
- Use ergonomic principles when designing the application of an LEV hood and make sure it is consistent with the way the worker actually does the job.
- Try out the LEV selected; make prototypes and get feedback from users.

- Use observation, information on good control practice and simple methods, eg smoke or a dust lamp, to assess exposure control effectiveness. Take measurements, eg air sampling, where necessary.
- Match the LEV control effectiveness to the potential degree of overexposure based on:
  - how exposure occurs; and
  - the capabilities of different hood types and designs.

101 For an individual process, increasing the degree of enclosure:

- improves the efficiency of the extraction;
- reduces the volume flow rate required to achieve the specified degree of control;
- reduces the running costs.

Control effectiveness

102 The effectiveness of an LEV hood can be reduced by flow separation and draughts. It is important to have an airflow indicator to make sure the hood is working properly.

Figure 15 Airflow into a hood

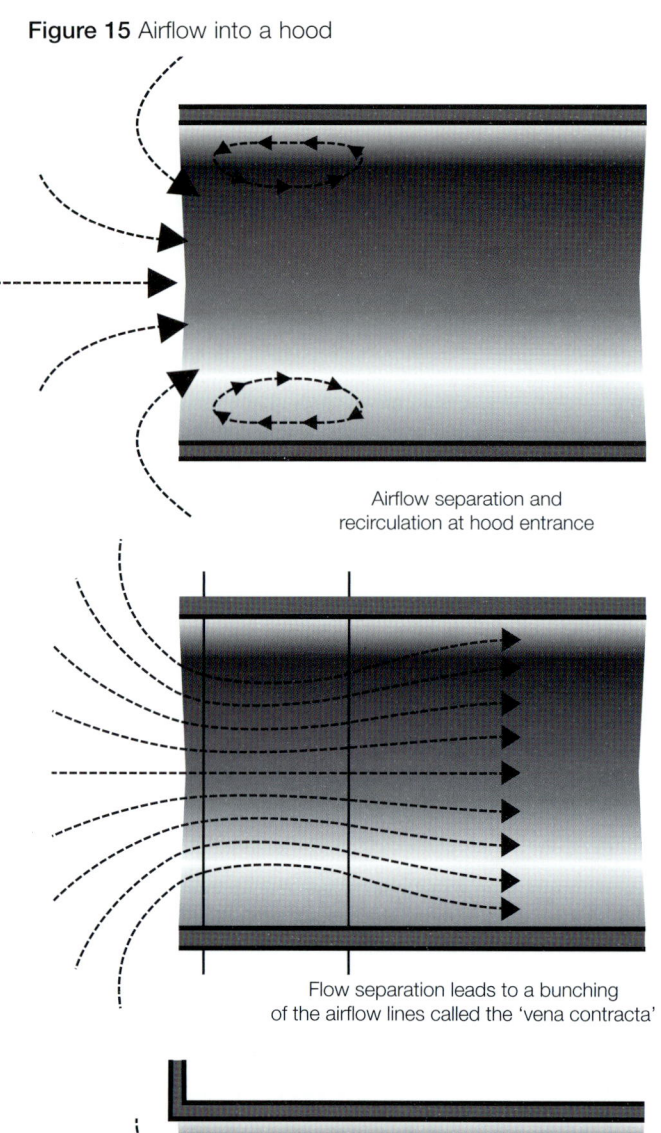

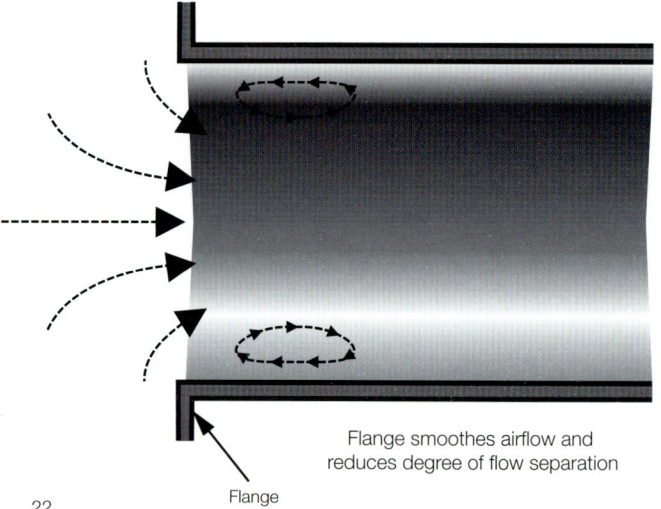

Airflow separation and recirculation at hood entrance

Flow separation leads to a bunching of the airflow lines called the 'vena contracta'

Flange smoothes airflow and reduces degree of flow separation

Flange

Flow separation

103 Where flowing air enters a hood, there is always some 'flow separation' and recirculation of air at the entrance edges. As the airflow enters an enclosure, the flow separates from the enclosing wall. The streamlines then become parallel – this region is called the 'vena contracta'. The greater the flow separation, and the more turbulent the airflow within the hood, the lower the hood efficiency. The flow separation and vena contracta can be reduced by smoothing the flow of air into the enclosure using a flange or flared inlet (see Figure 15).

Draughts

104 Draughts can reduce the effectiveness of hoods and have many causes, including:

- turbulence from other processes nearby;
- the natural effects of windy weather;
- cooling fans;
- open doors and windows;
- vehicle movements;
- workers moving around nearby;
- poorly planned make-up air.

105 A hood needs a minimum face velocity to resist draughts, or contaminated air can spill out from the hood. In industrial settings, draughts can reach up to 0.3 m/s. Consequently, a hood face velocity of at least 0.4 m/s is required in most workrooms to overcome the effects of draughts. Shallow hoods and capturing hoods are particularly sensitive to draughts. Draught assessment requires observation, the use of smoke and an anemometer.

Airflow indicators

106 Employers need an airflow indicator at every hood because the operator needs some simple indication that the hood is working properly. It becomes critical when the operator has to adjust a damper to get adequate airflow. The airflow indicator must indicate simply and clearly when the airflow is adequate. The simplest indicator is usually a manometer. (Also see 'LEV instrumentation' in Chapter 7.)

107 The rest of this chapter examines the types of hood in more detail. A set of design principles follows the description of each type of hood.

Enclosing hoods

Full enclosures

108 In full enclosures, the process and the source are within the hood, however large. Examples of full enclosures include glove box, isolator or reactor. Total enclosure does not necessarily mean complete isolation – there will need to be provision, for example, to allow replacement air to be drawn in, for materials handling, sampling, or filter changes.

109 The enclosure acts as a 'holding volume'. Good design ensures that disturbances in pressure caused by the process cannot lead to spillage of contaminant out of the hood. The pressure inside the enclosure must always be lower than that in the workroom outside the enclosure. The enclosure should be large enough to maintain negative pressure and contain any sudden release of contaminant. The design principles are in Table 4.

'Room' enclosures

110 Room enclosures contain the operator and the process and are totally enclosed. They are frequently referred to as booths, rooms or cabins and may be named to describe the process which takes place inside them, eg abrasive-blasting booth, paint-spraying cabin, isolation room, or clean room. Such enclosures are available commercially. The main objectives of these enclosures are to:

- contain the contaminant cloud to prevent other employees being exposed;
- reduce the process operator's (the employee's) exposure;
- discharge cleaned air to atmosphere.

Table 4 Full enclosure: Design principles

Enclosure	Predict the maximum source size and make the enclosure large enough for the contaminant cloud. Make the enclosure large enough to maintain negative pressure and contain any sudden release of contaminant. Minimise the impact on walls and ensure the cloud is directed away from openings and entrance ports. Minimise gaps in the fabric of the enclosure. Make hinges, seals and fixings robust. Plan the inlet port and filter sizes. Provide an alarm in case of overpressure.
Airflow	Select an extraction flow rate to exceed the maximum volume flow rate from the source. The pressure differential should be large enough to draw replacement air through gaps in the enclosure body or through entry filters, and minimise leakage of contaminated air.
Usability	Design for long-term working by operators of different sizes. Should be comfortable and usable, eg with lighting inside (or from outside) the enclosure, and transparent inspection panels. Locate process instrumentation outside the enclosure. Provide visible monitoring instrument displays and accessible controls. Liaise with supervisors and process operators. Design for a clearance time, after which interlocks on the enclosure will release.

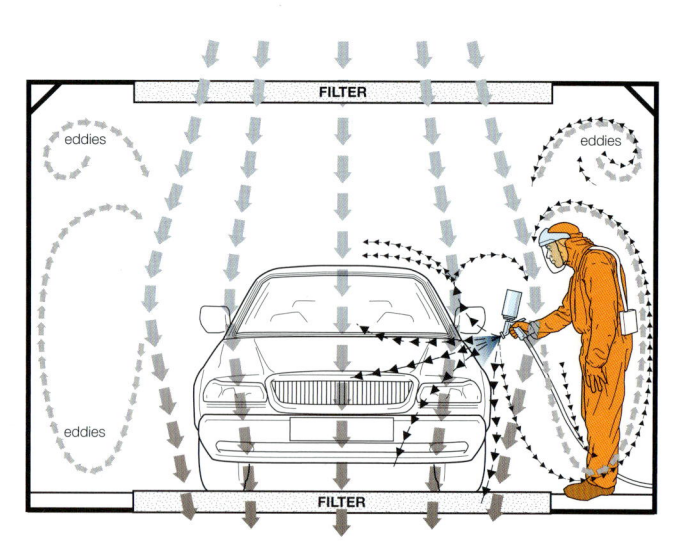

Figure 16 Spray booth or enclosing room

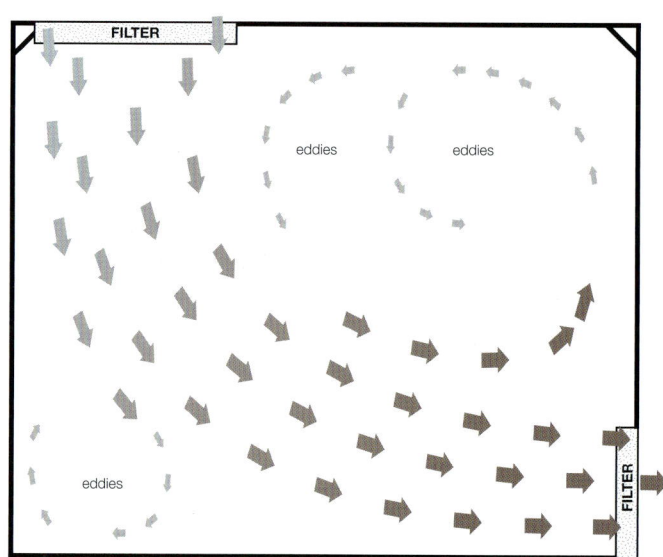

Figure 17 Cross-flow room

111 Ventilation may be:

- downward (downdraught or vertical airflow), where clean air enters through a diffuser that covers, or nearly covers, the ceiling. It exhausts through the floor, eg Figure 16; or
- cross-flow (cross-draught or horizontal airflow), where clean air enters through diffusers that partly cover a wall. It exhausts through filters in an opposite wall or the floor, eg Figure 17; or
- hybrids of these.

112 Effective designs maximise 'piston' or one-way smooth airflow. However, this objective is not often achieved.

113 The inward and outward airflows should balance to produce a slightly lower pressure than that outside the room. In most rooms, the airflows induce large-scale eddies.

Clearance time

114 The clearance time of room enclosures is frequently overlooked. A considerable time may elapse between shutting off the source and the air in the room being fit to breathe. The more persistent the eddies, the more they will retain the contaminant, and the longer the clearance time. The exposures of process operators are greater when clearance times are long. Good practice requires that:

- the designer should minimise the clearance time;
- airflow within the room should not stop until the clearance time has elapsed;
- people using enclosing rooms should know how to get in and out safely. The room may need an entrance vestibule;
- the 'LEV commissioner' needs to establish or confirm the clearance time (see Chapter 8). The time must be displayed and everyone concerned should be told.

115 Workers in room enclosures often need effective respiratory protection. Where necessary, the designer should make provision for respiratory protective equipment (RPE) that needs a clean air supply, for example air plug-in points in the room, near the pedestrian doorway. The design principles for room enclosures are in Table 5.

Partial enclosures (booths)

116 Partial enclosure is a compromise between containment and accessibility. The advantages over capturing hoods are:

- the physical enclosure of the walls and roof can reduce the volume rate needed for effective control;
- the source is shielded from draughts;
- the source (and sometimes the complete process) is within the hood and capture is not required;
- the airflow dilutes and displaces the contaminant cloud.

117 Enclosing hoods can control exposure more effectively than capturing hoods, but they may require relatively large volumes of air. Replacement or make-up air needs careful planning (see Chapter 7).

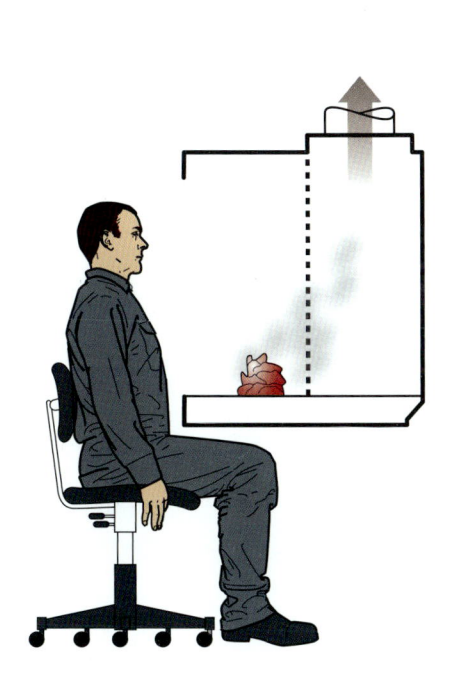

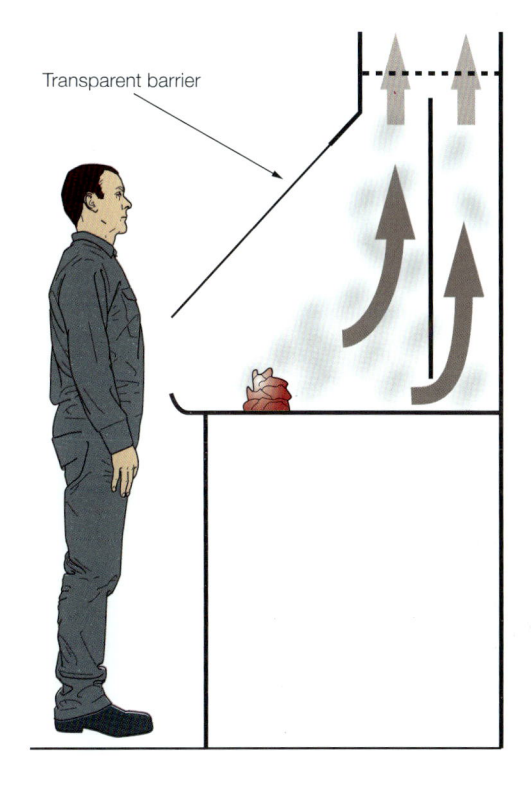

If the booth is too shallow, hot contaminant clouds can escape due to eddies and wake effects.

Figure 21 Partial enclosure: Ventilated welding bench

Figure 22 Open-fronted booth with transparent barrier

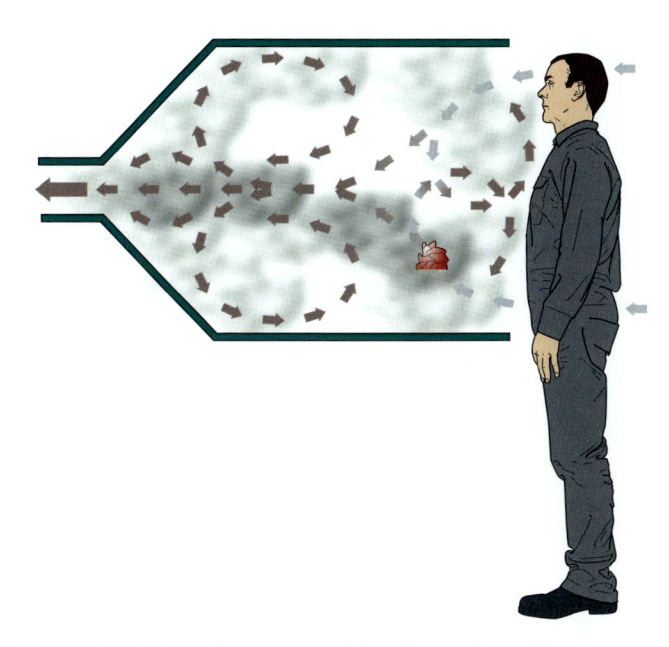

Figure 23 Wake effect at a small enclosure (booth) – the source is too close to the hood face and the operator

Move source away from hood face and operator

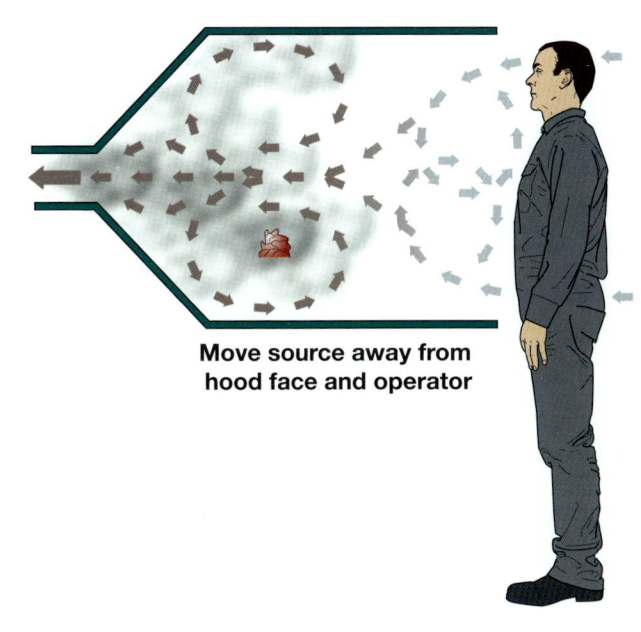

Figure 24 Move the source away from the hood face and operator

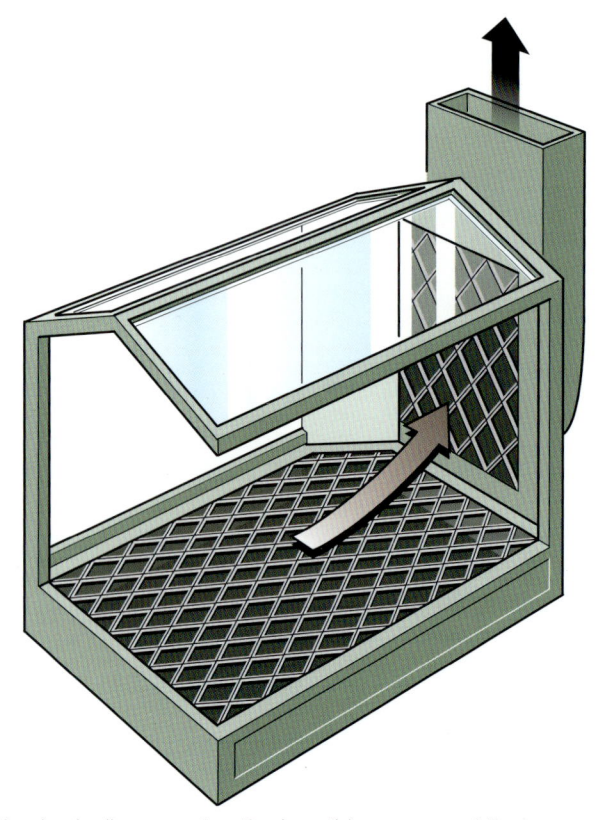

This physically separates the breathing zone and the source, and the side-draught minimises the creation of the wake in front of the operator.

Figure 25 Reducing wake effect using a side-draught hood

Figure 26 Reducing wake effect using a downdraught walk-in booth

Receiving hoods

125 All receiving hoods work on the same principles:

- The process takes place outside the hood.
- The contaminant cloud is propelled into it by process-induced air movement.
- The hood, especially the face, must be big enough to receive the contaminant cloud.
- The extraction empties the hood of contaminated air at least as fast as it is filled

Canopy hood

126 A common form of receiving hood is the canopy hood placed over a hot process to receive the plume of contaminant-laden air given off. It is important to separate the rising plume from the operator's breathing zone. For cold processes with no thermal uplift, canopy hoods are ineffective. Canopy hoods do not protect the operator who needs to work above a hot process (see Figure 27).

Canopy hood design and application

127 The hood receives the expanding cloud. It should be placed as close as possible to the process to intercept the cloud before it grows through mixing. This also reduces the cloud's susceptibility to draughts, as does partial enclosure at the sides and back. Low-level hoods (less than 1 m from the source) are easier to design and are likely to remove a high percentage of contaminant.

128 As a design rule of thumb, the extract rate should be 1.2 times the volume flow rate of the rising plume at the face of the hood. The overlap over the source area should be 0.4 times the height above the source.[13]

Other receiving hoods

129 A receiving hood can be applied wherever a process produces a contaminant cloud with a strong and predictable direction. For example, a grinding wheel, like all rotating discs, acts as a crude fan. The guard acts as a fan casing and directs the air jet mainly in the direction of the wheel rotation (see Figure 28). The receiving hood must be large enough and close enough to intercept the contaminant cloud (invisible) and the jet of fast-moving large particles (visible). The design principles for receiving hoods are in Table 7.

Table 6 Partial enclosure: Design principles

Enclosure	Characterise the source – its size, the contaminant cloud volume flow rate and its velocity. Make the enclosure large and deep enough to contain the source and the contaminant cloud. Design to minimise operator exposure. Design the hood entrance to create an even flow of air. Eliminate the wake effect, eg use downdraught, side-draught or work sideways-on to the airflow. Mitigate the wake effect, eg place the source further away from the operator, place a transparent barrier between the source and the operator's breathing zone or use local air displacement. Minimise obstructions inside the hood, especially near the entrance. Locate to minimise the influence of external draughts. Minimise the hood face open area with adjustable openings to the hood where feasible, eg a fume cupboard sash.
Airflow	Design the face velocity to be sufficient to contain the contaminant cloud, ie a minimum of 0.4 m/s unless a lower face velocity is shown to be effective. Choose a volume flow rate able to clear the hood of the realistic worst-case volume flow rate of contaminant cloud. Locate the process and workstation to direct the contaminant cloud into the hood. Design the enclosure to create even airflow at the face and within the hood. Anticipate any fall in performance, eg from a filter blockage. Design to minimise eddy formation.
Usability	Design the enclosure and work methods based on good ergonomic principles, eg for access and materials handling. Study methods of working and redesign in liaison with the operator and supervisor. Prepare prototype designs. Recommend jigs and tools that help the task. Provide a display of adequate airflow, eg a manometer, on the hood duct to measure and display static pressure. Design for use of RPE if operators require it. Provide lighting inside the enclosure.

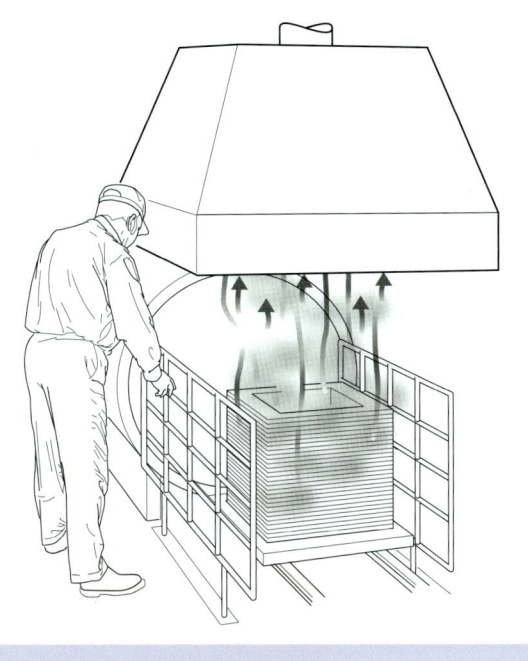

Good control design	Poor control design - the operators must work in the plume

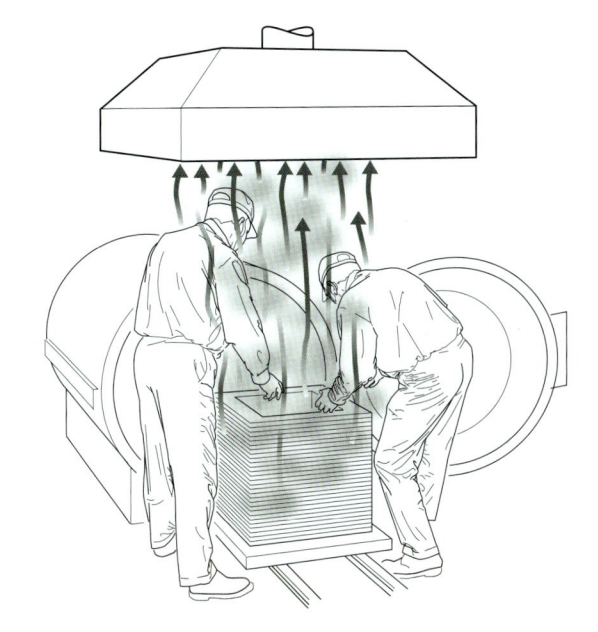

Figure 27 Canopy hoods over a hot process

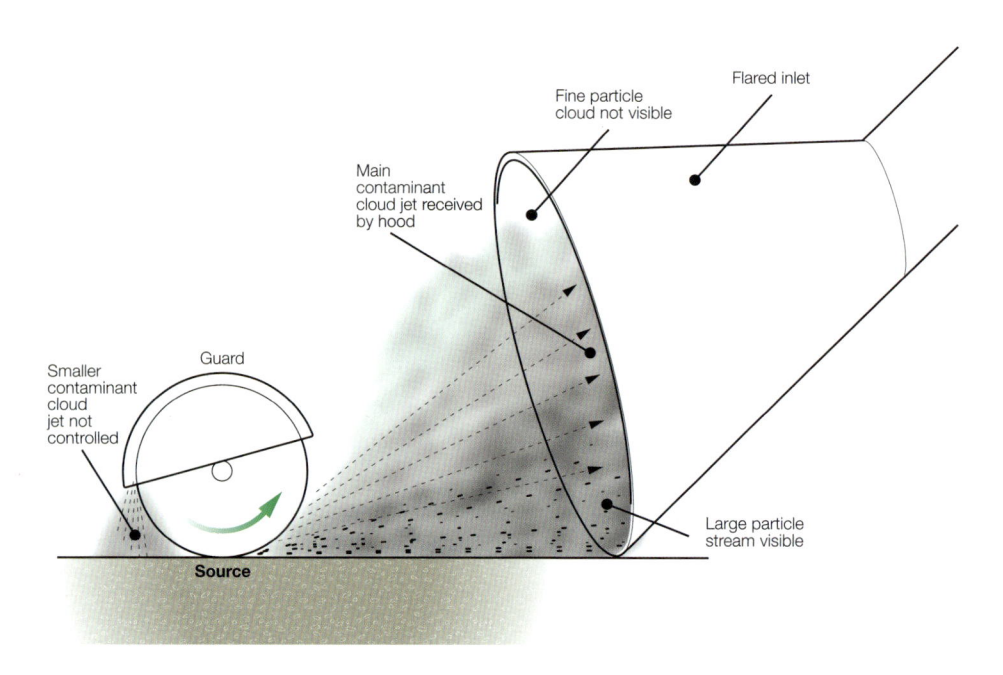

Figure 28 Grinding wheel and receiving hood

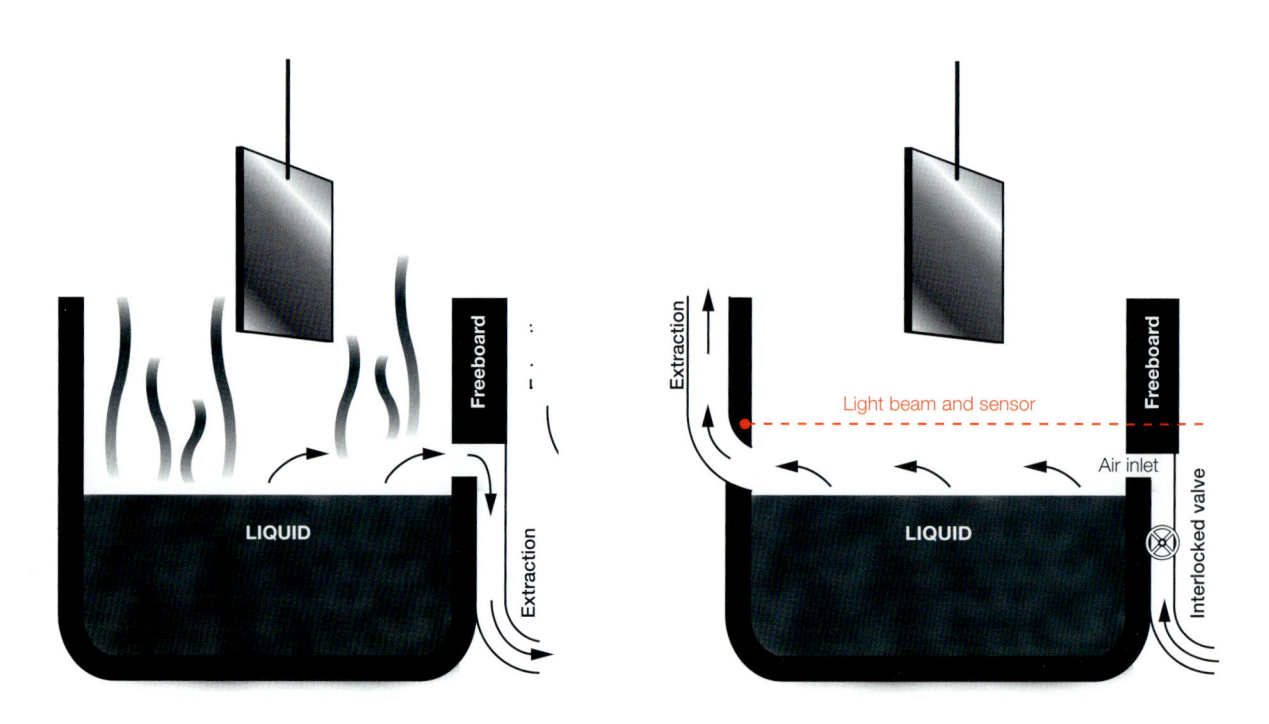

The tank is too wide for capture slots to be effective (left) while push-pull ventilation can be effective (right). Air blows from the slot across the tank towards the receiving hood, carrying and entraining the contaminant cloud.

Figure 29 Push-pull applied to an open-surface tank

Table 7 Receiving hood: Design principles

Location	Design the process layout so that the contaminant cloud flows towards the hood. Avoid or suppress draughts, especially for hot, relatively slow-moving, plumes. Place the hood as close to the source as possible. Can the hood be incorporated in machinery guarding, eg a partial enclosure?
Hood	Provide a hood with a large enough area and shape to hold the maximum volume flow of contaminated cloud. Assess the variation and realistic worst-case volume flow rate of the whole contaminant cloud, not just that visible in normal lighting. Make it visible, eg with a Tyndall beam or smoke. Receiving hoods are inappropriate controls for sources with little or no directional air movement or thermal lift. Select a different LEV hood design, eg a partial enclosure, if operators are exposed to the contaminant cloud, or design the workstation for the use of supplementary RPE.
Airflow	Design the volume flow rate to empty the hood at least as fast as it fills, to contain and remove the worst-case contaminant clouds.
Usability	Provide an airflow indicator, eg a manometer, on the hood duct to measure and display static pressure. Design the hood and work methods based on good ergonomic principles. Liaise with process operators and supervisors.

Push-pull system

130 Push-pull ventilation uses an air jet to blow contaminant-laden air that has little or no velocity towards an extraction hood. It converts a capturing hood into a receiving hood. Push-pull systems are inappropriate where, for example, draughts or process components can divert the push jet. The design principles are in Table 8. Push-pull systems are appropriate when:

- enclosures or an overhead canopy would block access or interfere with the process;
- an operator needs to work over a process emitting a contaminant cloud;
- a tank is too large for capture slots to control vapour or mist contaminant clouds.

131 The receiving hood should be designed so that it:

- is large enough to intercept the whole of the contaminant cloud;
- is located in line with the push jet;
- has a volume flow sufficient to empty the receiving hood at least as fast as it is filled.

132 For example a push-pull system may be the right control solution for an open surface tank. They also have uses for large area, low energy sources such as laminating glass-reinforced plastic with styrene-containing resins.

133 For large articles lowered into and raised from the tank, the designer should provide:

- an interlock to turn off the inlet air jet when a workpiece is raised or lowered. Otherwise, the jet of contaminated air is diverted by the workpiece into the workroom;
- means to control vapour from articles that may be wet with solvent, eg a tank freeboard or drying hood.

Table 8 Push-pull systems: Design principles

Location	Design the work process and the blowing jet so that the contaminant cloud flows predictably towards the receiving hood. Avoid or suppress draughts. Consider vapour controls for drying articles (tank dipping).
Inlet jet	Design to deliver air/contaminant jet exactly to the receiving hood. Experiment and use smoke or other means to check on the size, direction and flow rate of the 'push' jet. Provide interlocks to turn off the jet where an object obstructs the receiving hood.
Receiving hood	Place as close to the source and jet as possible and make sure it is large enough to receive the contaminant cloud jet. Maximise the source enclosure.
Airflow	Design to empty the hood at least as fast as it fills. The extracted volume flow rate must exceed the inlet air jet volume flow rate.
Usability	Provide an airflow indicator, eg a manometer, on the jet air supply to indicate appropriate airflow and a manometer on the hood duct to measure and display static pressure.

Capturing hood

134 The process, source and contaminant cloud are outside the capturing hood. This has to generate sufficient airflow at and around the source to 'reach out', 'capture' and draw in the contaminant-laden air. Capturing hoods are also known as exterior, external or captor hoods: they have a number of common names including slot and ventilated bench. The design principles are in Table 10. A capturing hood may be appropriate when the process cannot be enclosed or the contaminant cloud has no strong **and** reliable speed and direction.

135 Capturing hoods may be:

- any shape but are commonly circular, rectangular or slot shaped;
- flanged or without a flange, or with a flared inlet;
- freely suspended, or resting on a surface;
- fixed, moveable or attached to mobile extraction units;
- small or large in size from a few millimetres to over half a metre in diameter and up to several metres long;
- applied to a process or built into equipment such as a hand-held tool.

136 Capturing hoods are widely used because:

- they may be easy to retro-fit;
- they often interfere less with the process;
- there are many suppliers of off-the-shelf systems.

137 For the great majority of sources requiring control, however, a capturing hood is much less effective than the designer intended because:

- the capture zone is often too small;
- the capture zone can be disrupted by draughts;
- the capture zone does not encompass the working zone;
- the nature of the task moves the working zone out of the capture zone;
- the capture effectiveness is over-estimated;
- there is a lack of information about the capture zone size.

138 All of these drawbacks have design solutions, but the optimum solution may be to choose or develop another type of LEV hood with a greater degree of enclosure. It is crucial that the key characteristics of 'capture' are fully understood both by the LEV supplier and the employer (see Figure 31).

Capture velocity

139 'Capture velocity' is the velocity required at a contaminant source to overcome the movement of the contaminant cloud and draw it into the hood. But this is meaningful only with a defined distance between the source and the hood. Fast-moving contaminant clouds are very difficult to control with a capturing hood. They normally require a partial enclosure or receiving hood. The capture velocities quoted in Table 9 are based on success through experience. In practice the designer and supplier should check and, where necessary, make prototypes.

140 The lower end of the range of capture velocities in Table 9 applies to:

- 'harmful'* and low toxicity materials;
- low usages;
- intermittent uses;
- larger hoods;
- some directional airflow towards hood;
- no draughts.

141 The upper end of the range of capture velocities in Table 9 applies to:

- 'toxic'* materials;
- high usage;
- continuous uses;
- smaller hoods;
- airflows away from the hood;
- draughts.

* 'Harmful' and 'toxic' are classifications under the Chemicals (Hazard Information and Packaging for Supply) Regulations (CHIP).[14]

Surface treatment: Ensure the hood is near the source

Fine fettling: Move the hood to follow the work

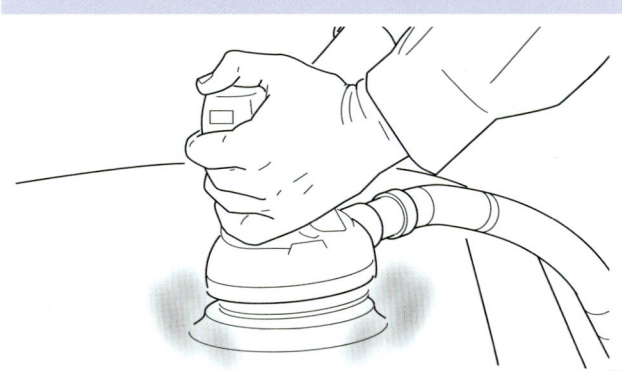

Sanding: Ensure the extraction is still working when the surface is curved

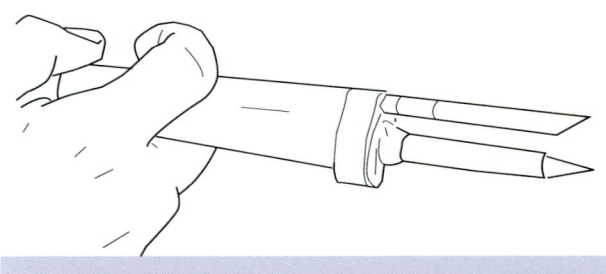

Soldering: Unblock this type of extraction regularly

Table 9 Capture velocities

Figure 30 Some capturing hoods

Contaminant cloud release	Example of process	Capture velocity range, m/s
Into still air with little or no energy	Evaporation, mist from electroplating tanks.	0.25 to 0.5
Into fairly still air with low energy	Welding, soldering, liquid transfer.	0.5 to 1.0
Into moving air with moderate energy	Crushing, spraying.	1.0 to 2.5
Into turbulent air with high energy*	Cutting, abrasive blasting, grinding.	2.5 to >10

* These types of cloud are difficult to control using capturing hoods.

Effective | *Partly effective* | *Ineffective*

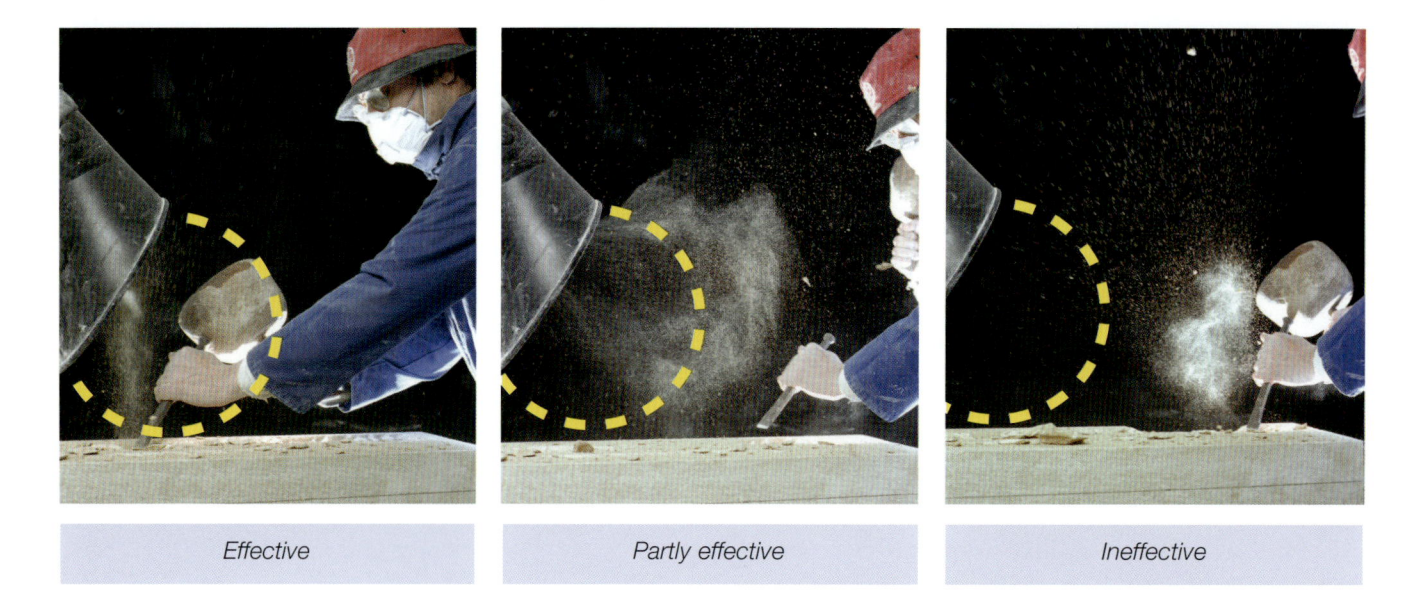

Figure 31 Capture zone and working zone

Capture zone, working zone and breathing zone

142 The capture zone of a capturing hood is the space in front of the hood where the air velocity is sufficient to capture the contaminant cloud. One way to envisage the capture zone is a 'bubble' in front of the hood. This 'bubble' is easy to disrupt – it can shrink and change shape. Draughts can severely affect the size and shape of capture zones, and powerful draughts virtually destroy them. Figure 31 shows a working zone within, partially within, and outside a hood's capture zone.

143 The capture zone is almost always smaller than the user expects. That is because the air velocity falls very rapidly in front of a capturing hood. As a rule of thumb, at one hood diameter out from the face of a capturing hood, the air velocity has fallen to about one tenth of the face velocity.

144 The working zone is the space where the activity generates the contaminant cloud. For effective exposure control, the working zone must lie within the capture zone of a capturing hood.

145 The breathing zone is the region around operators from which they draw air for breathing (commonly defined as being within 300 mm of the nose or mouth).

Distance from the source

146 Capturing hoods will nearly always be ineffective when placed more than a hood diameter away from the source. The shape of the capture zone depends on the hood's shape. The effective capture zone is severely limited, particularly for small hoods.

147 Measurements show that the degree of effectiveness of a capturing hood decreases sharply as the distance from the hood increases. All capturing hoods show this capture pattern. The smaller the hood, the smaller the 'partly effective' region. In practice, capturing hoods either capture or they don't: the difference between these two states is a small change in the work position. It is common to find that capturing hoods do not capture contaminant effectively – sometimes, they do not capture contaminant at all.

148 Process operators need to know the size and shape of the capture zone so they can work within it. Suppliers and designers of capturing hoods need to provide information on the capture zone of their hoods in a practical way, for example:

- clearly mark out the capture zone on the workstation; or
- mark the hood with the maximum capture distance.

Moveable working zone

149 Some work processes are 'linear', in that the activity and source move along a workpiece or component, eg applying adhesive, seam welding. When applying capturing hoods to such activities it is imperative to keep the working zone within the capture zone, by using an adjustable hood or an adjustable workstation. However, this is often impracticable and, if so, another type of hood or control is needed.

Capturing hood flanges

150 The airflow contours for a capturing hood extend around the back of the hood. With the source at the front of the hood, such airflow is 'wasted' – it has no effect on control. Flanges on capturing hoods:

- restrict the movement of air from behind a capturing hood;
- create a larger capture zone and a longer 'reach' in front of the hood;
- improve the air velocity distribution – the flow into the hood is smoother, with less eddying and this increases the hood 'entry coefficient', making it more efficient.

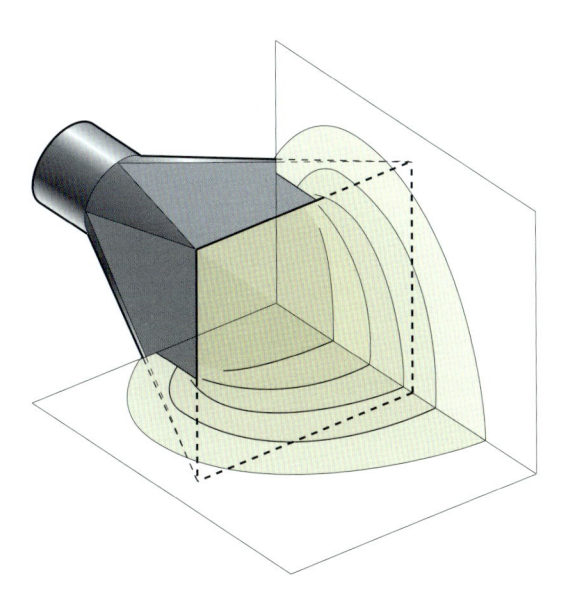

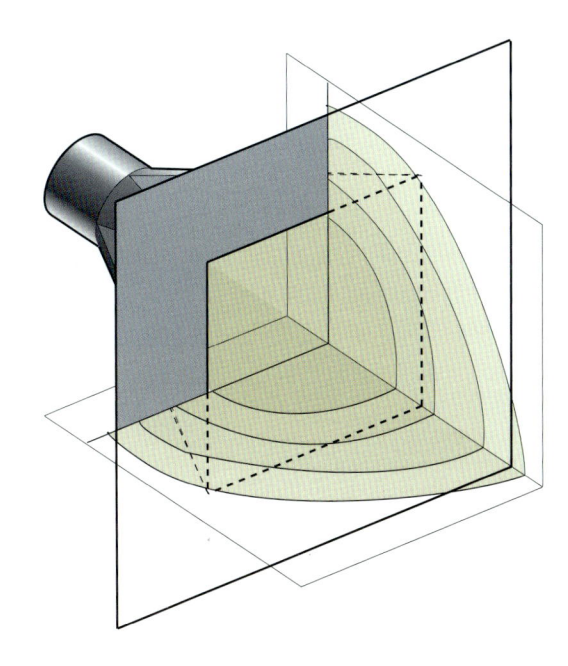

Note: the relative effectiveness of a flange increases as the hood aspect ratio increases, ie flanges have a greater effect with a slot-shaped hood.

Figure 32 The effect of flanges on capture hood velocity contours

151 Figure 32 shows this effect with a square section capturing hood.

Specific examples of capturing hoods

Rim or lip extraction

152 This is extraction along one or more sides of a source such as a tank with an open surface. A slot (a long, narrow hood) is required to extend along the length of the source. However, the capture zone for a slot is very limited, and where there are slots down both sides of a tank, the capture zones need to meet in the middle.

153 As a rule of thumb, surfaces up to 0.6 m wide require a slot along one side, and surfaces between 0.6 and 1.2 m wide require slots down both sides. Control of a wider surface is impractical using rim or lip extraction – controlling emissions needs a different solution.

Downdraught table

154 Holes or slots extract air downwards through a horizontal surface. Downdraught tables are usually used where the contaminant is generated close to the table surface. The working zone is at, or very near to, the table or bench top. As a rule of thumb, the air velocity at the face of the hood should exceed 0.3 m/s. Very high face velocities can result in high noise levels.

155 Downdraught tables and benches:

- can only capture contaminant clouds released with low energy or downwards, ie processes such as plasma cutting, and not processes such as disc cutting;
- may be unsuitable for objects that cover more than a small area of the table.

156 With walls and even a ceiling, the downdraught table is more like a partial enclosure and becomes more effective.

LVHV

157 Some industrial tools, such as grinding wheels, have a rapidly moving surface. These surfaces also carry with them a layer of air moving at high speed (a boundary layer). Fine dust particles can be carried in this boundary layer and, because of the high speeds involved, they can be difficult to capture.

158 Low volume high velocity extraction (LVHV) involves a small hood with a high face velocity, eg 100 m/s, located very close to the source. Typically LVHV is applied in hand-held tools, but can be used with fixed equipment.

159 LVHV can be built into a rotary sander to successfully control the escape of dusty air (see Figure 30). It is difficult to retrofit LVHV. Designers of hand-held equipment that incorporates LVHV must apply ergonomic principles for user-acceptance and successful control.

Table 10 Capturing hood: Design principles

Location	Locate as close to the source as possible, normally less than one hood diameter away. The capture zone should be large enough to encompass the working zone. The capture zone should be defined, marked on the workstation and/or indicated on the hood labelling. Avoid or suppress draughts. Consider making prototypes.
Hood	The shape of the hood should be similar in size and shape to the source and contaminant cloud. It should be flanged or have a flared inlet with further enclosure where possible.
Airflow	Adequate to create a large enough capture zone.
Usability	Define and mark out the capture zone. Design a moveable, adjustable hood or moveable workstation to keep the working zone within the capture zone. If not practical, provide a different control solution. Provide a visible display of adequate airflow such as a manometer on the hood duct. Design the hood and work methods based on good ergonomic principles.
Draughts	Move the hood and source closer together, eg use a more enclosing hood. Increase the volume flow rate.

7 Designing the rest of the system

Key points

- The system must work to its specified performance and withstand wear and tear.
- The system components should be easy and safe to check, inspect, clean, test and maintain.

160 This chapter describes the rest of the system and the work environment.

Introduction

161 Chapter 6 discussed the size, shape, design and placement of the hood. It explained how the extract air velocity and volume are critical to a hood's success. The 'job' of the rest of the LEV system is to extract the right air volumes from the hood(s). There are key issues to address when designing the rest of the system, such as ductwork, air movers, air cleaners, and discharge to atmosphere and air recirculation.

Design

162 The rest of the LEV system should conduct the contaminated air away for cleaning or discharge. In all but simple systems, the design of LEV systems should be 'iterative', developing through the design process. The designer should:

- plan the layout – the initial design;
- specify the volume flow from each hood in a custom design;
- establish the flow rate and total pressure at each junction;
- plot the design in standard-size ductwork;
- recalculate the flows to establish where these deviate from the initial design;
- adjust the flows to the required values using tapers or slide valves;
- recalculate to generate a 'system curve' to show the volume of air moved through the system for any given pressure at the air mover. (Also see 'Fan characteristics' in paragraphs 197-201.)

163 Calculations that may be useful for designers can be found on the HSE website (www.hse.gov.uk/lev), eg:

- air density – adjustment for temperature;
- air velocity from pressure difference;
- circular duct cross-sectional area;
- maximum vapour concentration for a liquid;
- conversions between Pa, ppm and mg/m^3 for vapours and gases.

Ductwork

164 Ductwork[15] connects the components of a ventilation system and conveys the contaminated air from the LEV hood to the discharge point. It consists of some or all of the following:

- ducting from the hood;
- dampers to adjust or balance the flow in different branches of the LEV system;
- bends, junctions and changes in the duct diameter;
- markings, including test points and hazard warnings of the duct contents;
- a connection to the air cleaner and air mover.

165 Usually all the above are under negative pressure (ie lower than that in the workplace). Ducting on the discharge side of the air mover will be under positive pressure (ie higher than that in the workplace).

166 Ducts can be either circular or rectangular in cross-section. Circular ducts are generally preferable because they:

- have a lighter structure for a given cross-sectional area;
- have a greater ability to withstand pressure differences;
- produce less noise, as there are no flat panels to act as secondary sources of vibration.

167 Designers should take the following points into account with regard to ductwork:

- Keep the design as simple as possible.
- Provide smooth-bore ductwork and an obstruction-free interior for particle extraction.
- Have a sufficiently high air velocity to keep particles suspended in the air stream, while low enough to keep noise levels acceptable – above 5 m/s air movement in ductwork starts to produce noise.
- Route ductwork to minimise noise nuisance.
- Keep duct pressures negative within the building, as far as possible.
- Have the minimum number of bends and junctions to minimise the flow resistance.
- When changes of direction are necessary, they should be made smoothly. Junctions and changes of section should also be smooth. Do not use T-junctions.

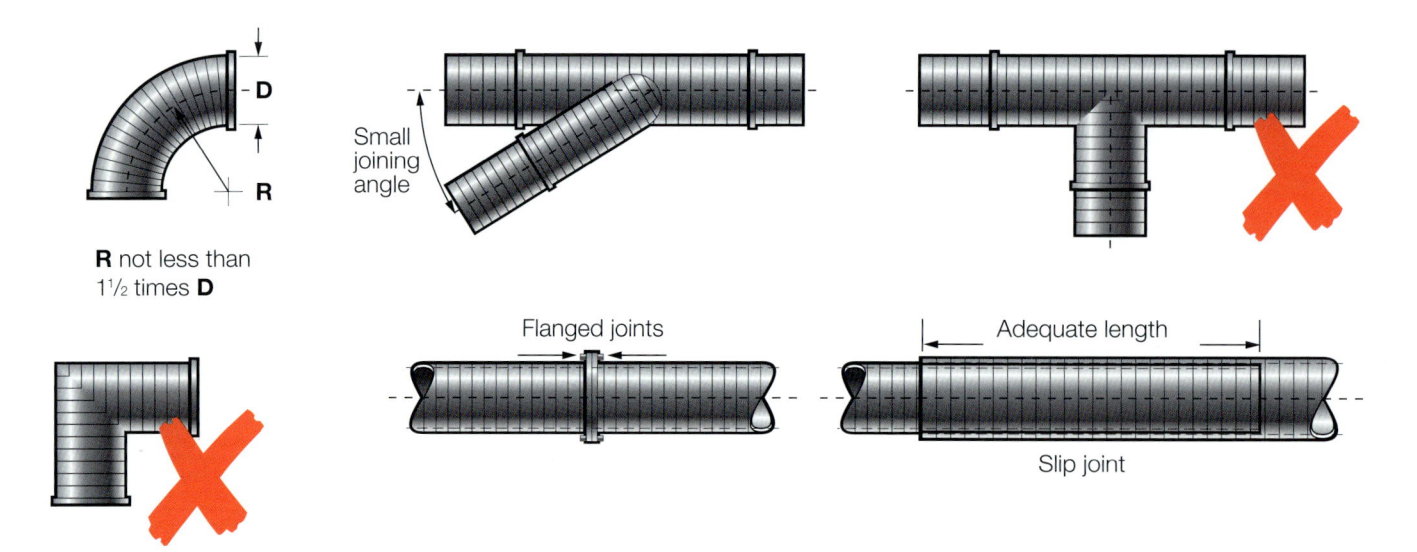

Figure 33 Bends, junctions and joints in ducting

- Incorporate tapered sections when the duct cross-section needs to change.
- Provide drainage points at any low points in an LEV system for aerosols, mists, or substances that may condense or support combustion.
- Provide access points as appropriate for cleaning and to clear blockages.
- Minimise the length of horizontal run for transport of particles.
- Depending on the expected range of temperatures, the ducting should accommodate thermal expansion and contraction.

168 Designers need to avoid:

- long lengths of flexible ducting, which have high flow resistance and low resilience. Flexible ducts can wear, split and are easily damaged;
- U-bends, as they cause particles to accumulate and block the duct.

169 Ductwork must not violate the fire compartments of the building.[16, 17]

Materials for duct construction

170 Taking into account the physical conditions and chemical nature of the contaminants, the materials should:

- give the best resistance consistent with cost and practicability;
- have sufficient strength and supporting structures to withstand likely wear and tear.

171 The wall thickness[18, 19, 20] should vary according to what the ducts will transport, for example:

- 'Light duty' ducts for non-abrasive materials (eg paint spray, mist, wood dust, food products, pharmaceuticals).
- 'Medium duty' ducts for non-abrasive materials in high concentrations, or moderately and highly abrasive materials in low concentrations.
- 'Heavy duty' ducts for highly abrasive materials (sand, grit, rock, fly ash). Consider providing 'sacrificial' units – easily replaced parts of the duct, eg bends.

172 Galvanised sheet steel is suitable for many applications, particularly at high temperatures. Coated mild steel may be required to resist chemical attack. These materials also give some degree of fire protection. For non-corrosive low temperature applications, aluminium or plastic (PVC, polypropylene) may be suitable. Table 11 recommends wall thickness based on durability.

Facilities for duct examination

173 Where appropriate, provide leak-proof inspection covers to facilitate inspection and cleaning inside ducts. These need to be accessible and simple to open.

174 Provide test points – as a minimum, 'static pressure tappings' in ductwork to monitor the system or to diagnose deterioration or partial blockages:

- after each hood or enclosure;
- at key points in the duct system;
- at certain components to measure pressure drops, eg across fans and filters.

Table 11 Ductwork wall thickness

Duct diameter in millimetres	Thickness in millimetres		
	Light duty	Medium duty	Heavy duty
0 to 200	0.8	0.8	1.2
200 to 450	0.8	1.0	1.2
450 to 800	1.0	1.2	1.6
800 to 1200	1.2	1.6	2.0
1200 to 1500	1.6	2.0	2.5

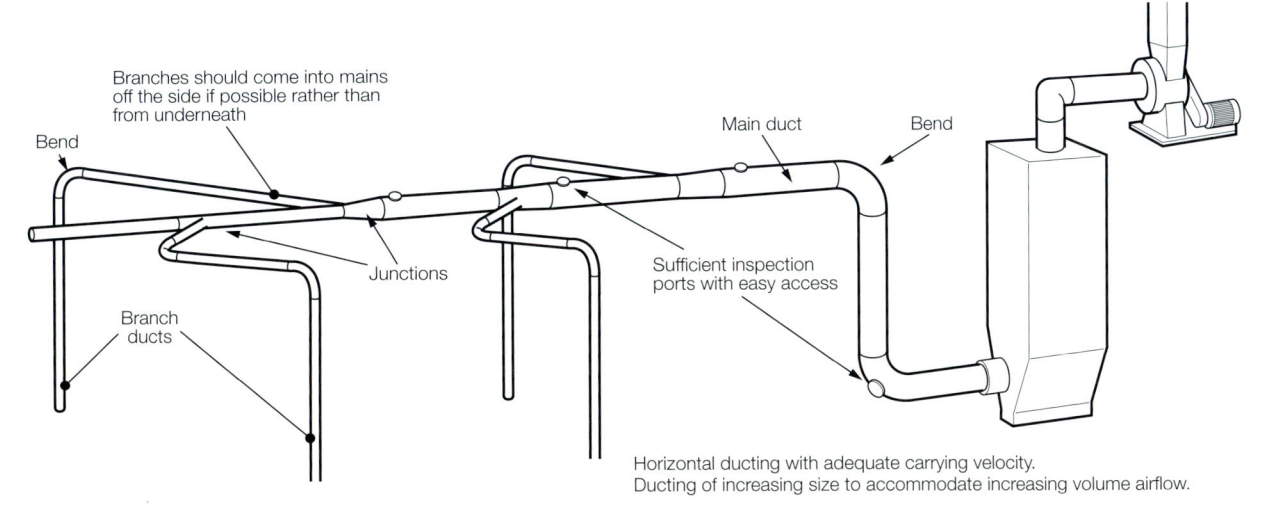

Figure 34 A multi-branch LEV system

175 Mark the ducts to show where these points are. Consider providing a suitable way to provide safe access to them.

Duct (transport) velocities

176 The air velocity through the duct must be high enough to keep particles suspended in the air stream. It should also be high enough to suspend and remove particles that settle out when the system stops. The designer needs to avoid deposition in any part of the ductwork. This is a particular problem:

- in long horizontal runs of ducting;
- at low points;
- at junctions where the duct diameter increases;
- after junctions or bends;
- when conveying large and small particles together, eg woodworking dusts.

177 Accumulation of settled particles reduces the diameter and shape of the duct, increases resistance and reduces the airflow in the system. Settled particles are difficult to re-entrain in the airflow and can lead to duct blockage.

178 The required transport velocity depends on the type of contaminant being conveyed. Table 12 recommends some minimum velocities.

Ductwork performance

Multi-branch LEV systems

179 The design should provide the required velocity to bring contaminated air from the hood furthest away from the air mover (either in terms of distance or system resistance) to the air mover. It is common for several hoods to feed into a main duct. The fan must have enough power to move air at the required velocity throughout the system when the maximum number of hoods is in use. To reduce cost, it is desirable to isolate unused hoods, eg using dampers.

180 Dampers give a degree of flexibility, but the system can easily get thrown out of balance if they are tampered with. For this reason, whenever possible, designers should avoid giving operators the control of dampers. For industries where dampers are common (eg in woodworking), operators need good information on damper use, and effective supervision.

Table 12 Recommended minimum duct velocities

Type of contaminant	Indicative duct velocity, m/s
Gases and non-condensing vapours	No minimum value
Condensing vapours, fume and smoke	Up to 10
Low or medium density, low moisture content dusts (plastic dust, sawdust), fine dusts and mists	Up to 15
Process dust (cement dust, brick dust, wood shavings, grinding dust)	Around 20
Large particles, aggregating and damp dusts (metal turnings, moist cement dust, compost)	Around 25

Varying the volume flow in the LEV system

181 Where the client anticipates changes in the volume flow rate, such as isolating unused hoods, the design options to cope with these changes include:

- a variable speed fan drive, where the fan speed varies to maintain a constant static pressure within the duct;
- fan belt or pulley drive changes, which requires technical intervention;
- dampers, which are not energy efficient.

182 See Chapter 8 for information on balancing an LEV system. This is highly skilled work, particularly for a multi-branch system.

Pressure losses

183 Every hood, duct element and air cleaner of an LEV system is associated with a 'pressure loss'. The designer should add up the pressure losses due to each component of the system to select a fan that will overcome the airflow resistance of the ductwork and the fittings. There are several ways of doing this, for example:

- 'American method': Treat bends and fittings as having a pressure loss equivalent to a certain length of straight ductwork.[13]
- 'British method': Treat the straight runs of ductwork separately from bends and fittings. The designer calculates the pressure loss for each component, added to the ductwork pressure loss. This calculation is made at a stated volume flow rate.[21]

184 Examples of how to calculate pressure losses can be found on HSE's website: www.hse.gov.uk/lev.

Connections between the ducting and fan

185 Air should enter and leave the fan as a uniform flow with minimum turbulence. Bends and junctions in ducting near the fan cause either swirling (on the negative pressure side) or increased static pressure (on the positive pressure side), which reduce efficiency. Ideally, bends on the discharge side of a centrifugal fan should be at least five duct diameters downstream.

Fans and other air movers

186 The fan is the most common air mover. It draws air and contaminant from the hood, through ductwork to discharge. There are five general categories of fan:

- propeller;
- axial;
- centrifugal;
- turbo exhauster;
- compressed-air-driven air mover.

Propeller fans

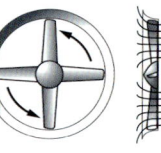

187 Propeller fans are often used for general or dilution ventilation. They are light and inexpensive to buy and run, with a wide range of volume flow rates. However, they will not produce much pressure and operate best against low resistance.

188 The fan blades are of sheet material (metal or plastic) mounted in a plate or cage and on a hub that is attached directly to the shaft of an electric motor, or belt driven. Generally, they are unsuitable for ducted systems with a moderate resistance or with particle filters.

Axial fans

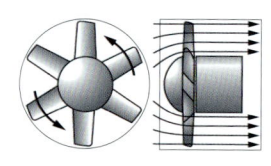

189 Axial fans are not suitable for dusts. They are compact, do not develop high pressures and cannot overcome the resistance to flow that many industrial applications require.

190 The impeller fan blades are on a rotating hub mounted in a short cylindrical casing. The fan is in the duct. Unless the contaminant is flammable or corrosive, the motor is also in the duct.

Centrifugal fans

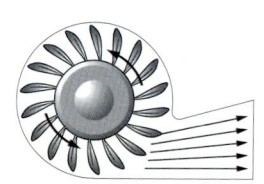

191 Centrifugal fans are the most commonly used fans for LEV systems. They generate large differences in pressure and can produce airflows against considerable resistance.

192 The impeller fan blades are mounted on a back plate, often within a scroll casing. Air is drawn into the centre of the impeller along the line of the drive shaft. The air is ejected at a tangent to the impeller.

Types of centrifugal fan

193 The blade shape characterises the type of centrifugal fan:

- Radial blade (most commonly, paddle type). These are robust, easy to maintain, clean and repair. They can convey heavy dust or product loads. Radial blades are often a solution for dusty contaminant clouds.
- Forward curved multivane. These have many relatively small blades. The blade tips incline towards the direction of rotation. Rotational speed is usually lower than with other types of centrifugal fan. Forward curved multivane blades may be unsuitable for dusty contaminant clouds.
- Backward bladed (curved, flat, laminar, aerofoil). These can overcome high system pressures. With high dust loads, dust can accumulate on the impeller which can lead to imbalance and vibration.

Turbo exhausters (multi-stage centrifugal)

194 Turbo exhausters can generate the high suction pressures needed to power low volume high velocity (LVHV) systems: they are not conventional fans. They use high-precision blades that are susceptible to damage by dust and require a filter to protect the exhauster.

Compressed-air-driven air movers

195 Compressed-air-driven air movers are appropriate where electrically powered fans are unsuitable, eg where access is difficult, or where there are flammable gases. They are small, inexpensive and easily portable. Their main disadvantages are the high running cost (compressed air is expensive) and high levels of noise for relatively small amounts of air moved.

Fan location

196 The objective is to have as much of the ductwork as possible under negative pressure. In particular, indoor ductwork upstream of an air mover should normally be under negative pressure. Leakage in this ductwork will then be inward and contaminated air should not escape into the workplace. One solution is to locate fans and positively pressurised ductwork outside occupied areas.

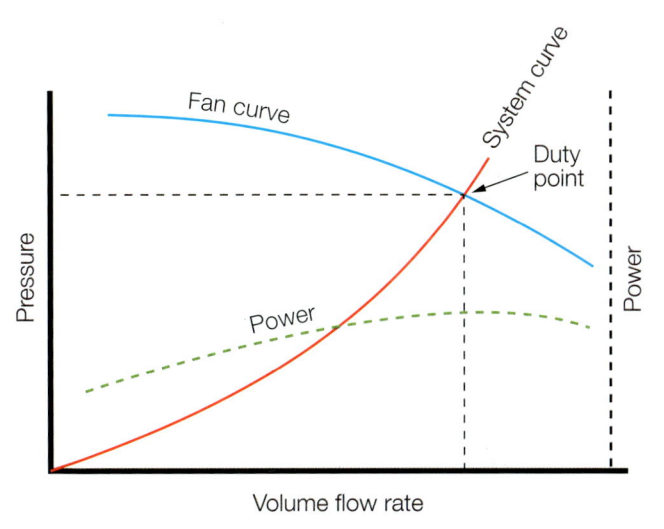

Figure 35 Fan curve showing intersection with system curve

Fan characteristics

197 The efficiency and noise characteristics of fans vary significantly between fan types, sizes, speed and how they are used. The power required from the fan, and its efficiency, vary with the volume flow rate. The curves of pressure, power and efficiency against volume flow rate are known as 'fan curves' (see Figure 35). Fan manufacturers' catalogues present these curves for each of their fans, and provide information to help the designer choose the right fan.

198 The 'system curve' shows the volume of air moved through the design for any given pressure at the air mover. The designer should select an air mover that is capable of moving at least this volume of air at that pressure difference – the fan curve.

199 The designer should select a fan so that system and fan curves cross at the design pressure and flow point (the duty point). It is often necessary to use a variable controller or restriction valve to move the fan curve so that this and the system curve cross where needed.

200 The 'duty point' gives data to specify the fan for the system – the pressure and power for the required volume flow rate. In fact, Figure 35 is rarely plotted: the duty point is selected from the system curve and a table of fan characteristics. However, a graph of the curves does show whether the duty point is in a stable area, ie whether minor leaks, blockages or defects would cause a drastic deviation in the system performance with a chosen fan.

201 It is important to ensure that the duty point is within the optimum range of the fan. Operation outside this range leads to an increase in noise and power consumption. That can overload the fan, leading to system failure.

Fan selection

202 For a particular application, many factors need consideration for fan selection. These include:

- the type of substance in the contaminant cloud;
- flammability or combustibility;
- the airflow required;
- the system resistance characteristics;
- the fan pressure characteristics;
- space limitations;
- the method of mounting the fan, and the type of drive;
- the operating temperature;
- acceptable noise levels.

203 More detailed information on fans, their application and selection can be found on the Fan Manufacturers' Association website (see 'Useful contacts') and in a joint CIBSE publication, the *Fan application guide*.[22]

Air cleaners: Particles

204 Particle collectors are the most common group of air cleaning devices associated with LEV systems. The group consists of fabric filters, cyclones, electrostatic precipitators and scrubbers.

Fabric filters

205 These are suitable for dry dusts. Dusty air passes one way through a fabric layer that is flexible and porous. The fabric may be constructed and treated to carry electrostatic forces which help attract and retain dust. Particles are removed by:

- impaction, where particles, larger than the weave, meet the surface of the filter;
- impingement, where medium-size particles meet the fibres within the filter weave;
- diffusion, where small particles are attracted towards the fibres.

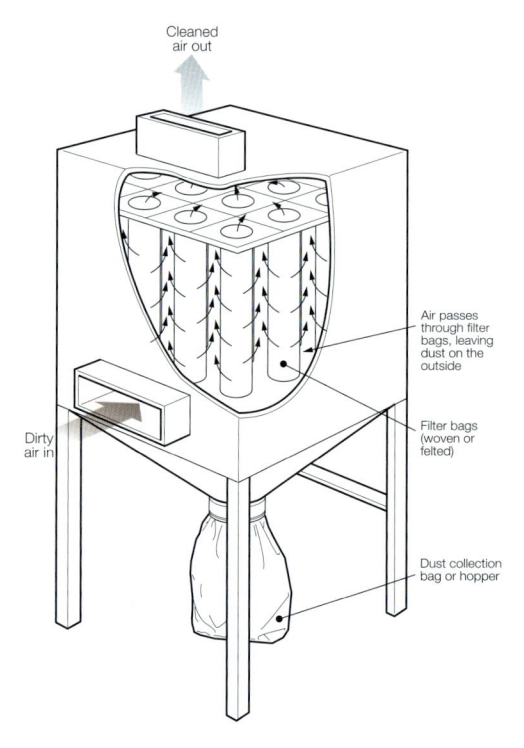

Figure 36 Bag filter unit

206 The main ways to clean filters are:

- mechanical shaking;
- reverse airflow; and
- pulse-jet.

207 The cost of the filter material is a major expense. It is also an operating cost, as filters need periodic replacement before they fail. The designer should specify the replacement interval, which is normally between one and four years.

Cyclones

208 Cyclones consist of a circular chamber, tapered at the bottom. Dusty air feeds at a tangent into the top of the cyclone and swirls around the chamber. This throws particles out to the wall by centrifugal action. The particles' velocities decrease and they fall to a collection hopper at the base of the cyclone. Cleaned air passes through a central outlet in the top of the cyclone. The larger the particle, the easier it is for a cyclone to remove it from the air.

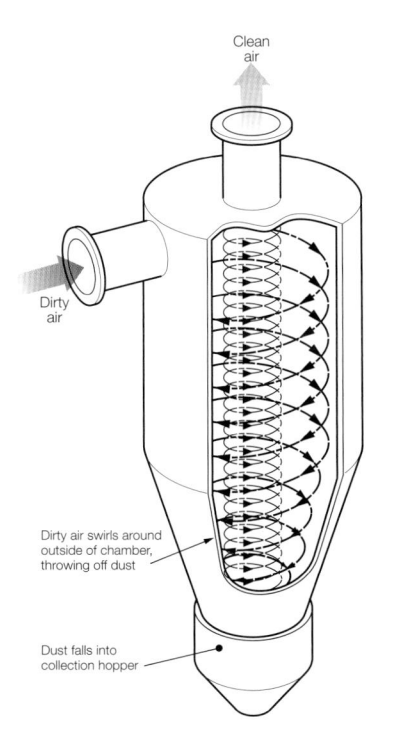

Figure 37 Cyclone dust separator

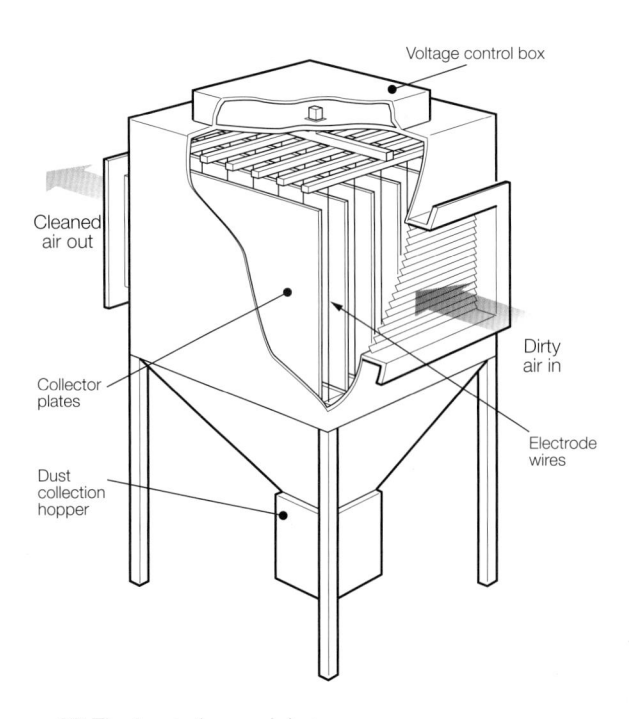

Figure 38 Electrostatic precipitator

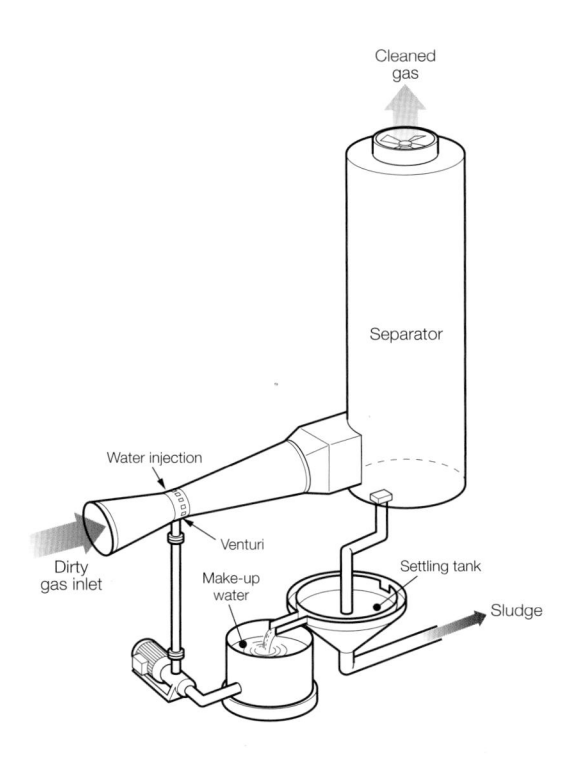

Figure 39 Venturi scrubber

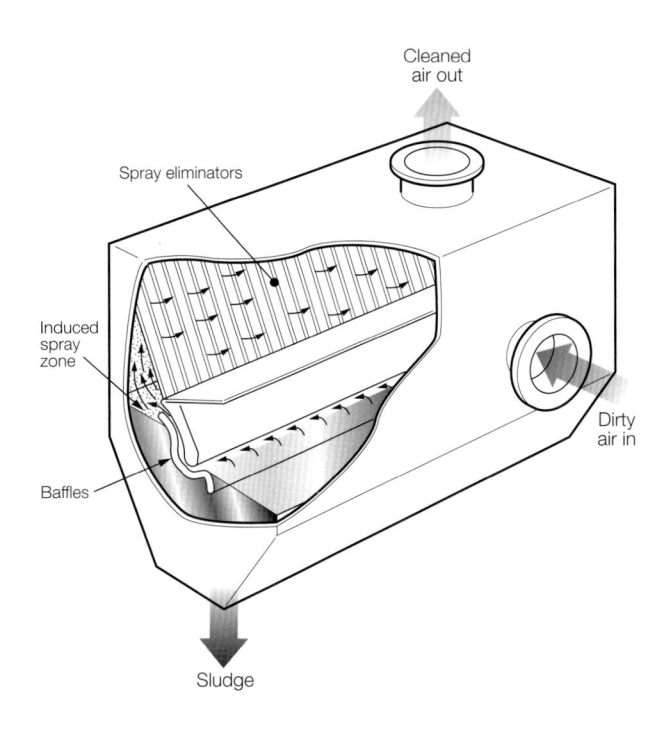

Figure 40 Self-induced spray collector

Electrostatic precipitators

209 Electrostatic precipitators are suitable for fine dusts, but unsuitable for heavy contamination. They give dust and fume particles an electrical charge and attract them onto collecting surfaces with an opposite charge. Cleaned air flows out of the device. There are two classes of design:

- pipe or tube, where a high-voltage wire lies along the axis of a grounded tube;
- parallel plate, where a series of high-voltage wires lie between a series of grounded metal plates.

Scrubbers

210 'Scrubbing' means wetting particles and washing them out of a contaminant cloud. The design requirements are to:

- wet the particles;
- cause them to settle out in water;
- provide a suitable disposal system;
- prevent dust building up at the inlet;
- prevent water carry-over in cleaned air.

211 There are numerous designs of scrubbers, the most common being venturi scrubbers, self-induced spray collectors and wet cyclone scrubbers.

Venturi scrubbers

212 Dusty air passes through a narrow venturi throat which has water injection. The conditions in the throat are highly turbulent. The water separates into small droplets that collide with the dust particles. A cyclone separates the droplets to produce a sludge containing the dust. Cleaned air passes through a central outlet in the top of the cyclone.

Table 13 Air cleaners – Particles

Type	Approximate collection efficiencies	Advantages	Disadvantages
Fabric filter	Can rise to over 99.9%	• Fabric filters increase in efficiency as the dust 'cake' builds up.	• Flow resistance increases as the dust cake builds – airflow falls. • Greasy or waxy materials can clog the filter permanently. • Abrasive materials cause rapid wear.
Cyclone	2 µm particle – zero 5 µm particle – 50% 8 µm particle – 100%.	• The pressure drop is small compared with other dust collectors. • Good efficiency for larger particles.	• Poor collection efficiency for small particles.
Electrostatic precipitator	1 to 5 µm – 80 to 99% 5 to 10 µm – 99%+	• High temperatures and corrosive conditions. • Fairly low running costs. • Low pressure drop (50 to 200 Pa).	• High investment cost. • Quite large. • Limited flexibility on changes in operating conditions. • Performance may be poor for particles with very low or very high electrical conductivity. • Shorting and sparking when very dirty. • Requires specialist cleaning.
Wet scrubber (venturi, spray collector, wet cyclone)	More than 5 µm – 96% 1 to 5 µm – 20 to 80%.	• Hot gases. • Removes sticky particles without clogging. • Eliminates fire and explosion hazards. • Dust-free disposal.	• High noise levels. • Corrosion. • Freezing in cold weather. • Disposal of slurry and polluted water. • Some dusts are difficult to wet. • Bacteria and bad smells.

Self-induced spray collectors

213 Dusty air is drawn under a baffle in a water trough. The dust impacts on droplets and also on water in the trough. A 'spray eliminator' or 'drift eliminator' separates water droplets from the cleaned air. The contaminant settles out as sludge at the bottom of the collector. To avoid bacterial infection and consequent bad odours, spray collectors need regular cleaning. There may be a legionella risk.

Wet cyclone scrubbers

214 Dusty air enters a cyclone collector that has a centrally located water spray directed outwards. The cyclone separates the droplets, producing sludge from the dust. Cleaned air passes through a central outlet in the top of the cyclone.

Air cleaners: Gases and vapours

215 The technologies used include destruction methods, packed tower scrubbers and recovery methods.

Destruction methods, such as thermal oxidation (incineration) or flare

216 Gases or vapour are destroyed before discharge by burning or thermal oxidation. Thermal oxidiser units can be fitted with heat recovery that partially offsets the fuel costs.

Packed tower scrubbers for substances that mix with water

217 A tower is filled with packing to provide a large surface area. Water or a reagent solution flows in at the top of the tower and contaminated air enters at the bottom. Trickling fluid absorbs the contaminant and cleaned air emerges at the top. To avoid bacterial infection and consequent bad odours, tower scrubbers need regular cleaning. There may be a legionella risk.

Recovery methods, such as adsorption

218 Contaminated air passes through filters that remove gases and vapours. Activated carbon filters are the most common. Air is usually filtered of particles before being passed through a carbon filter. Regeneration of carbon filters and solvent recovery is feasible, but recovery becomes viable only when the solvent usage is high. Impregnated carbons are able to absorb specific chemicals. Typical disadvantages include:

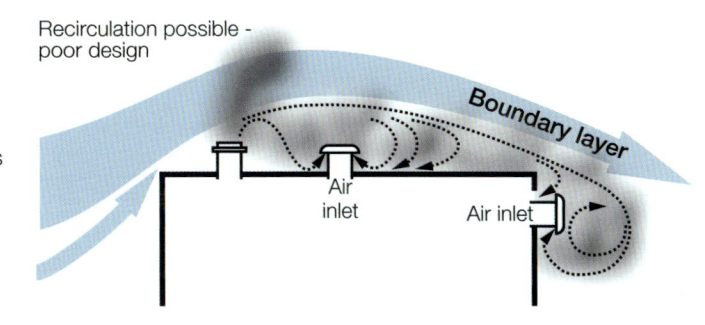

Low discharge stack relative to building height
Air inlets on roof and wall

Figure 41 Location of discharge stack

- a frequent need to change the filter;
- the filter fails suddenly when saturated; and
- carbon can develop 'hot spots' that need detectors and fire-extinguishing systems.

219 Caution: charcoal filters are **not** particle filters.

Discharge to atmosphere

220 Whether or not it has been cleaned, extracted air must not re-enter the building or enter other buildings unless the contaminant has reached negligible concentrations. Discharged air must leave the discharge duct at a high enough speed to make sure it is dispersed. Discharge is normally via a 'stack'.

Stack siting

221 Buildings have a surrounding 'boundary layer' of air. The objective is to discharge air beyond the boundary layer, and prevent it entering recirculation eddies. The discharge point should be located well above the highest point of a building.

222 The designer needs to know the airflow patterns around a new installation's building, ie:

- the recirculation eddy produced by the leading edge of the roof;
- the downwind wake;
- the effect of wind direction.

Stack design

223 Gas leaves a discharge stack and rises due to its momentum and buoyancy. Once its energy has decayed and the air cooled to ambient temperature, the plume is carried by the prevailing wind.

224 Increases in the velocity of the final discharge can be achieved by putting a tapered nozzle on the outlet. Taller stacks prevent the mixing of discharged air with the boundary layer air, but these may not gain planning approval. The Environment Agencies (EA, SEPA) or local authorities may have stipulations for stack height.

225 Other ways of increasing the plume velocity are:

- grouping exhausts into fewer stacks; or
- placing exhausts very close together so that plumes merge.

226 Avoid rain caps and other devices that reduce upward vertical velocity. Never use the 'Chinese hat' or other devices that direct the discharge downwards (see Figure 42a).

227 The employer may need a permit from the environmental regulator for discharges to the atmosphere. There are separate Pollution Prevention and Control (PPC) Regulations in England and Wales, Northern Ireland and Scotland (see www.netregs.gov.uk).

LEV instrumentation

228 Users of LEV systems, particularly the operators at LEV hoods, must be able to tell that the hood airflow is still adequate to control exposure. Good practice requires the periodic monitoring of performance for all hoods. The designer should therefore specify suitable monitors such as manometers or other airflow indicators.

Airflow indicators

229 Airflow indicators cover a wide range of equipment:

- a simple and reliable device such as a manometer connected to the hood duct. The static pressure is a direct indicator of the airflow rate;
- a complex device, eg a pressure switch to activate an alert if the flow drops below pre-set trigger levels (see BS EN 14175-2:2003 *Fume cupboards. Safety and performance requirements*[23]).

(a) Never use this type of discharge

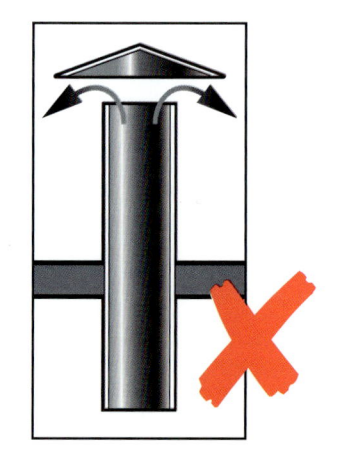

(b) Alternative with better discharge characteristics

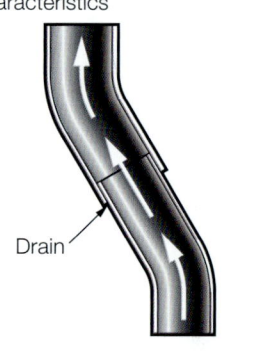

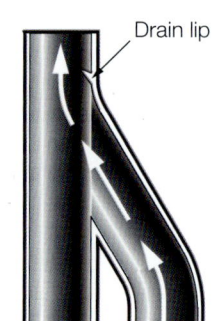

(c) Off-set discharge stack

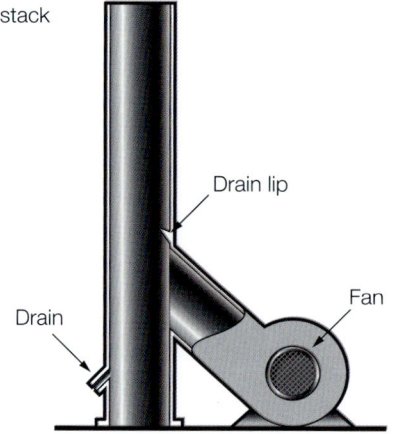

Figure 42 Stack design

Manometers

230 Manometers are pressure gauges that indicate 'static pressure'. They come in several forms:

- electronic (pressure transducer);
- mechanical (pressure-sensitive diaphragm), which requires no power, and is safe for flammable atmospheres;

- liquid in glass, which requires no power, is safe in flammable atmospheres, and is cheap and precise. The disadvantages are that air bubbles may form in the liquid, or the liquid may evaporate.

Alarms and indicators

231 Alarms can fail without warning. It is good practice to specify in the user manual the frequency of alarm testing. The designer needs to specify the appropriate intervals between tests for alarms and indicators.

Work environment and process issues

Recirculation of extracted air

232 Recirculating extracted air is a way to save energy and reduce heating or cooling costs. It also reduces the need to consider make-up air. Recirculation is easier with:

- contaminants which are particles;
- low concentrations of airborne contaminant compared with the 'benchmark' value (Chapter 3);
- relatively small LEV systems; and
- lower toxicity materials.

233 The air cleaner is the most important part of a recirculation system. It must match the contaminant and its concentration. Recirculation is acceptable as long as the air is thoroughly cleaned. Recirculation may be inappropriate when failure of a component, such as an air cleaner, could result in dangerous conditions. Under these circumstances, any recirculation system must incorporate monitoring and alerts, for example:

- an alarm for a blocked or failed filter, eg a pressure gauge for continuous monitoring;
- an advanced detection system connected to alarms and a system to divert recirculated air out of the workplace.

234 Testing of detectors and alarms is vital and must be covered in the user manual (see Chapter 9).

Recirculating fume cupboards

235 Recirculating fume cupboards that are used to control dust, mist or fume should be fitted with a high efficiency particle arrestor (HEPA) filter. The filter seating needs to be checked every time it is changed, and the system needs continuous monitoring.

236 Recirculating fume cupboards that use adsorption filters are not recommended because it is not possible to predict when the filter is likely to fail, and it is uneconomic to install a suitable monitor, eg a flame ionisation detector (FID).

Make-up or 'replacement' air

237 Extracted air needs planned replacement, otherwise the room would be at negative pressure or have severe draughts. The LEV would not then perform as designed. Make-up air is an integral part of an LEV system and heating it is an important running cost. The volume of make-up air must match the volume of air extracted. For small LEV hoods in large workrooms, natural ventilation may provide enough make-up air. For large LEV hoods in small workrooms, fit passive or active inlet vents.

238 Typical signs of an inadequate supply of make-up air include:

- fumes from a naturally-ventilated flue enter the workplace;
- doors opening out of the workplace are difficult to open;
- doors opening inwards are difficult to close;
- draughts whistle under doors and through window frames;
- the fan may become more noisy;
- the flow through the hood increases on opening a door or window;
- a pilot light on a gas appliance may go out.

239 One common cause of make-up air supply failure is stacked materials or rubbish blocking inward air vents.

240 Make-up air should not create draughts or disturb the airflow into an LEV hood. Designers should size openings to minimise such effects, and site them away from hoods.

General workroom ventilation

241 LEV might not be the right control solution when:

- there are a large number of widely-spaced sources;
- the source is large and LEV is impossible to apply over the entire source;
- the source position is not fixed;
- the source emits relatively small amounts of contaminant;
- the contaminant is offensive but not harmful.

242 The employer, working with the designer, may decide to have LEV to control the main sources and use general ventilation for minor sources or any loss of contaminant from large sources. General ventilation involves replacing contaminated workplace air with cleaned or fresh air. Dilution or mixing ventilation and displacement ventilation are two forms of general ventilation.

Dilution or mixing ventilation

243 Clean air dilutes contaminated workplace air by mixing with it. The assumption that the concentration of contaminant is uniform throughout the workplace is common but usually wrong. In practice, mixing is incomplete because there will be some areas with high local concentrations in the workplace, usually near sources.

Displacement ventilation

244 Clean air pushes contaminated air away with minimal mixing. This 'piston' or 'plug' flow can be produced by:

- introducing air at an even rate over a whole wall, displaced through the opposite wall;
- supplying air at a low point in the room that is a few degrees cooler than the workplace air. Warmer contaminated air displaces upwards for clearance (eg via louvres);
- supplying warm air at a high level and venting contaminated air at a low level.

245 For displacement ventilation, the clean air's velocity should be high enough to maintain a uniform flow and low enough to avoid general mixing. Caution: successful large-scale displacement ventilation is difficult to achieve.

Special case: Local air displacement (LAD)

246 Local air displacement is not LEV since it does not extract air. It is appropriate for work in a defined and limited zone, where other controls do not deliver an adequate reduction in operator exposure. LAD is a wide, slow moving jet which supplies clean air to the operator's breathing zone, entering over a plenum. The flow entrains contaminated air at the edges, but the jet is wide enough to keep the contaminated air away from the operator's breathing zone (see Figure 43a). A high-speed narrow jet has a clean air core that will not extend to the operator's breathing zone and so is inappropriate (see Figure 43b).

247 LAD is not designed or intended to blow away contaminant clouds and is not suitable for contaminant clouds from hot processes. It can be used alone or combined with an LEV system. The design principles for LAD are in Table 14 and the key features are:

- The air supply should be as close as practicable to the operator's breathing zone, but not be so close as to cause discomfort or restrict movement.
- The downward airflow must counteract any upward flow of air caused by the work process. The flow should be smooth, at around 1 m/s over the face of the plenum, with no swirling.
- The working area should be limited to the core of clean air which should be large enough to cover the working area.
- Ideally, LAD air should be at or slightly below the temperature of the workroom air. In cold working conditions, the designer should provide for radiant heaters to maintain thermal comfort.

Other issues

Noise

248 The employer should specify the acceptable noise level and the designer needs to meet this specification. Noise generated by LEV can cause problems, especially where ambient noise is low. The noise originates from:

- fans – the type of fan, blade design, drive, bearings, mounting, casing, sound insulation and duct connection;
- turbulence in ducts, particularly flexible ducts, bends, changes in cross-section, high velocities and large particles;
- around small, high-velocity capturing hoods;
- noise created elsewhere, propagated by hoods.

249 Where appropriate, the designer should supply:

- anti-vibration mountings and sound insulation for fan assemblies;
- silencers or sound insulation for ducts;
- hoods designed so they do not generate excessive noise. As a rule of thumb, the air velocity at any air entry slot should not exceed 10 m/s.

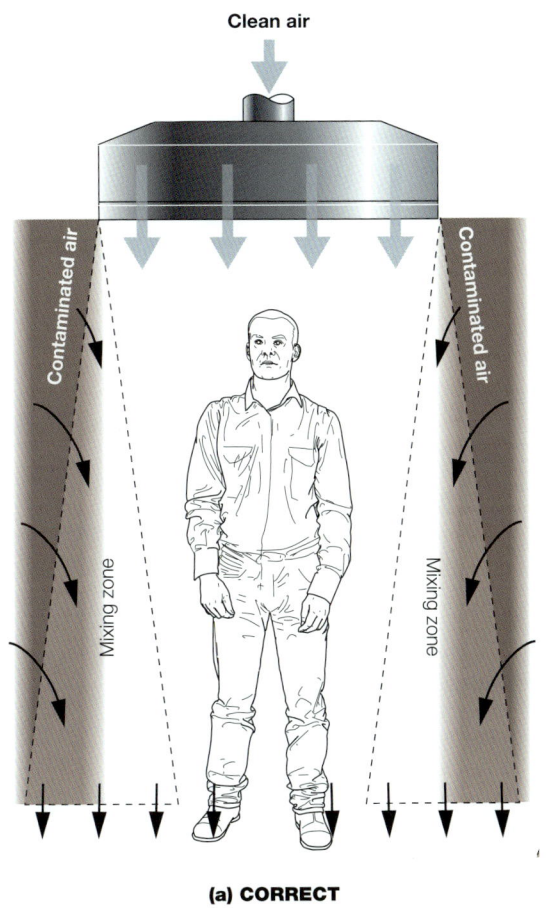

(a) CORRECT
Wide air jet, low speed
Keeps contaminated air away from
the operator's breathing zone

(b) INCORRECT
Narrow air jet, high speed
Small clean core, contaminated air is
in the operator's breathing zone

Figure 43 Local air displacement

Table 14 LAD: Design principles

Issue	Potential solution
Is LAD an appropriate option?	Consider process changes and LEV first.
Well-defined working zone	Design LAD to cover the whole working zone. Clean air must encompass the breathing zone during the task. Minimise draughts.
Positioning	Locate the plenum close to the operator's head.
Airflow design	Airflow should be sufficient to maintain a clean air core – 1 m/s at the plenum face may be adequate. Airflows should be even, with no swirling or eddies.
Design uncertain	Prototype the installation and test – iterative design.
Usability	Locate airflow indicator near the plenum duct. Radiant heaters may need to be available under the operators' control.

Thermal comfort

250 The air inlets should be designed to avoid creating cold draughts. It is important to 'temper' or take the chill off make-up air. This is a particular issue for work inside a booth with a large airflow rate and a light workload. An alternative to tempering may be to provide radiant heaters that are under the operator's control.

Lighting

251 Depending on the type of work, the employer should describe the need for lighting at the task. The supplier's design should meet this requirement.

252 Hoods reduce light and can make it difficult for the operator to see what they are doing. This can result in:

- the hood being moved aside, becoming ineffective; or
- the operator working outside or at the face of a booth, reducing its effectiveness.

253 Always design lighting for partial enclosures and walk-in booths. Consider designing a light source within moveable hoods.

Access

254 The designer should incorporate the need for operator access. These needs include routine work activity, inspection, cleaning, testing, maintenance and repair. If access is difficult, it is less likely that the employee will carry out these necessary duties and so the LEV system performance will degrade.

Work operations

255 Operators need to move equipment into the hood easily or to move the hood to the process easily. They need to be able to manipulate objects during working and, for walk-in booths, to be able to work around the object. The designer may consider specifying a turntable or jig for easier positioning of the work.

Inspection, testing, cleaning, maintenance

256 The operators require safe and easy access to:

- inspection doors of a reasonable size;
- hatches for ducts liable to blocking or fouling;
- the air cleaner, eg for changing filters, emptying the waste hopper, drainage and sludge removal;
- fans and drives that require parts replacing.

Table 15 The rest of the LEV system: Design principles

Location	Design for quiet running indoors.
Ducting	Provide airflow indicators, eg manometers, at hood ducts and at other necessary points. Minimise bends and smooth junctions. Make corrosion-resistant where necessary. Include drainage points for liquid from mists. Design as much of the duct as possible to run at negative pressure. Anticipate wear points, and plan for easy replacement. Include access to clear blockage points.
Airflow	Design for quiet running. Smooth airflows and particle transport. Deliver adequate make-up air. Discharge to a safe place.
Usability	Make sure there is safe and easy access to necessary parts of the system. Take noise, lighting and thermal comfort into account. Keep a stock of replacement parts.

8 Installing and commissioning

Key points

- The four stages for commissioning are installation, performance checks, assessment of control effectiveness and reporting.
- Testing and proving is critical.
- Existing LEV systems with no documentation must show effective control, and have performance data measured and recorded.

257 This chapter describes the points to cover for installing and commissioning LEV.

Commissioning

258 'Commissioning' is proving that an LEV system is capable of providing adequate control. The supplier's quotation to the specification (see Chapter 5) lists the essential features for adequate control. These need installing and commissioning to be effective in practice. Certain parts of the commissioning process used to be referred to as 'initial appraisal' and 'intended operating performance'. This book does not use those terms, but it incorporates their meaning. It also sets out a way of commissioning an undocumented LEV system where there is no user manual or logbook.

259 The employer is responsible for effectively controlling exposure by means of adequate control measures, both 'hardware' such as LEV, and work practices. This means:

- process-related equipment, eg seals, jigs, handling aids, as well as the LEV system;
- work practices, such as optimum work position, the angle and position of work tools and the correct use of the LEV.

260 Commissioning should cover both 'hardware' and work practices. LEV installers and commissioners turn equipment supplied to a design into hardware that provides adequate control of the hazard as specified by the employer as the client.

261 Effective commissioning requires the employer to work closely with the LEV supplier and LEV service providers. Service providers must tell the employer that installation and commissioning may interrupt production.

262 There are four stages to LEV commissioning:[24]

- installation (if necessary), and verifying that the system was installed as designed;
- showing that the LEV system meets the specified technical performance;
- control effectiveness – demonstrating adequate control of contaminant clouds;
- reporting readings as benchmarks for subsequent examinations and tests.

263 The LEV commissioning report, together with the user manual (Chapter 9), is the basis of the statutory 'annual' thorough examination and test.

Stage 1: Installation

264 The installer may be the design or supply company, the service provider, or even the employer (if competent). Further information on 'competence' requirements for LEV installers appears in Chapter 2 and Appendix 1.

265 The installer needs to organise the following before installation:

- footings for heavy items of plant;
- power supplies;
- compressed air supplies;
- safe access;
- the co-operation of the employer and the employer's staff.

266 For simple systems, installation is generally limited to unpacking, assembling, checking that ducts are clear (eg free of packaging), and turning on and initial adjustment. For more complex systems, installation should involve:

- a completeness check, to ensure all components were supplied, of the right type, size and rating;
- verifying power and other service facilities (eg compressed air) and checking they are sufficient;
- constructing the LEV system;
- checking the assembly is correct, with testing and access points identified;
- checking all components are in good working order and the air mover fan is turning in the correct direction;
- rough balancing with any dampers set;
- remedy of any simple faults.

267 The installer should report any undocumented or missing parts, and all modifications. Where there are problems installing the system as specified, the employer (as the client) and the designer or supplier must endorse any variations. For example, ductwork should not be 'shoehorned in' because of unforeseen space restrictions.

268 The process of installation may introduce health and safety hazards such as:

- work at height;
- manual handling;
- vehicle movements;
- machinery;
- fume from any welding;
- flammable atmospheres;
- electrical hazards;
- asbestos (encountered unexpectedly during work on the building fabric) – ask to see the client's Asbestos Management Plan.

269 The installer should discuss with the employer and agree how such risks are to be controlled. This book does not discuss these in further detail, but HSE has produced other publications which do (see www.hse.gov.uk). The Construction (Design and Management) Regulations 2007 (CDM)[7] may apply to the installation of LEV plant.

Balancing the system

270 The design of any LEV system with more than one hood needs each branch to extract just the right amount of air. Installation involves much more than simply connecting up the ducts and turning on the fan. Balancing[13, 15, 25] means achieving the performance required at every hood in a system. This must be done either by the installer, or by the commissioner. The airflow in each branch is determined by:

- inlet or hood resistance;
- duct branch length, diameter and flow resistance;
- flow conditions at the junction with the main duct.

271 Balancing is always required on installation, commissioning and on any reconfiguring of the LEV system. The correct balancing (and rebalancing) of an LEV system is a highly skilled activity, particularly on a multi-branch system. Altering the airflow in one duct affects the flows in all of the other branches. It is often necessary to work through the whole LEV system, and repeat the process at least once.

272 A common reason for an existing system to be seriously unbalanced at inspection is that somebody has isolated a redundant inlet, or added new hoods without recalculating the system. Balancing requires starting at each hood and branch, and making adjustments while working towards the air mover. ANSI also has standards for this (see 'Further reading').

273 Caution: It is a mistake to rectify serious imbalances using just dampers. This can cause local areas of dust or liquid deposition and wastes power.

Table 16 Principles of installation

Specification	Needs to be clear and unambiguous.
Installation	Meets the specification. Follows safe working practices – CDM may apply. Variations need to be agreed with the designer. Check thoroughly before handover for commissioning.

Stage 2: Technical performance

274 The new system must perform to the standards and benchmarks that the employer specified and for which the LEV supplier quoted. All systems need commissioning, and recommissioning, when there are:

- changes in the process;
- changes in the workplace layout;
- any changes of the equipment creating the source;
- any other changes such as modifying a branch or adding a new branch.

275 Information on 'competence' for LEV commissioners appears in Chapter 2 and Appendix 1.

Large systems

276 Certain large systems, for example those commonly found in woodworking, are specified to connect to more hoods than the air mover and cleaner are designed to extract simultaneously. Many hood ducts have 'blast gate

dampers' to isolate hoods that are temporarily unused. It is most important that the system and its limitations are well documented and that the user is trained to use these dampers. The supervisor needs to know which duct combinations may be open at the same time. This information should be displayed in a plan or diagram.

Technical performance testing

277 The LEV commissioner uses various assessment methods. The outcome of observation, testing and measurement is the commissioning report. This sets the benchmarks and standards against which the employer compares the results of statutory testing (see Chapter 10). It also sets the benchmarks for tests in the logbook for the system. The tests include measurements of:

- the volume flow rate at various points in the system including hood faces (where appropriate), hood ducts and the main duct;
- static pressures in various parts of the system including hood ducting, and across the filter and fan;
- hood face velocities (where appropriate);
- the fan speed, motor speed and electrical power consumption.

278 The tests could also include:

- replacement or make-up air supply;
- air temperature;
- filter performance.

279 The test records and calculations should enable easy comparison of volume flow rates, velocities and pressures with the specification. Where the system fails to deliver its design performance, detailed investigation and testing may be needed to reveal the causes of, and remedies for, the problem.

Stage 3: Control effectiveness

280 There are three general categories when assessing the effectiveness of LEV, although these can overlap:

- LEV of a design known to be effective;
- LEV design proven qualitatively to be effective;
- LEV design that appears to be adequate but control effectiveness is uncertain.

LEV of a design known to be effective

281 This is a proven, well-characterised LEV system, known to control exposure adequately. Such systems must be:

- of a standard design;
- applied to standard processes in an industry;
- made to clear design specifications.

282 The commissioner should record the observed and measured performance data in the commissioning report. Where LEV effectiveness depends on operator behaviour, ensure that the correct ways of working are also described. The data should appear in a commissioning report, and benchmark data should be entered in the logbook for the system.

LEV design proven qualitatively to be effective

283 This is when the LEV system is shown to provide the required protection, based on a careful observation of contamination sources and the hoods applied to them. When the system is examined using tests, such as smoke or a dust lamp, it works well. Such systems are less well characterised than 'LEV systems of a design known to be effective'. They need more careful commissioning, involving:

- close observation of sources and operator activities;
- smoke tests with the process running, with observation of smoke leakage, eddying and smoke encroachment into the operator's breathing zone;
- where the contaminant is dust or mist, dust lamp observation of the cloud behaviour with the process running;
- operator behaviour and the usability and sustainability of the control systems, observing that they are following agreed work methods.

284 Record all the LEV data that deliver adequate control, including the static pressure reading on every hood manometer. Where LEV effectiveness depends on operator behaviour, ensure that the correct ways of working are also recorded. The data should appear in a commissioning report and benchmark data should be entered in the logbook for the system.

285 A sub-set of this group is where the LEV appears to be effective, but there are no commissioning data available, no user manual and no logbook for the system. The commissioner then needs to make measurements of pressure and airflow data for a new logbook.

LEV design that appears to be adequate but control effectiveness is uncertain

286 This is often the case where an LEV system must give stringent control, eg for toxic substances. The system may be operating at its design limits. Where LEV is not effective enough, the client may need a different control solution that may not involve LEV (eg a refuge). Process operators and workers nearby may require respiratory protective equipment.

287 Where control needs to be stringent, observational checks alone are insufficient to judge adequate control. Measurement is also needed, such as air sampling.

Qualitative assessment methods

Observation

288 The experienced commissioner is able to judge the likely effectiveness of systems by simple observation. However, the judgement requires testing and the findings need to be recorded. Observation includes judging the adequacy of make-up air. Inspection within ducts etc requires an endoscope, fibre-optic camera or boroscope.

Making particle clouds visible

289 'Tyndall illumination' makes fine particles visible. The 'Tyndall effect' is the forward scattering of light. This is commonly seen when a shaft of sunlight entering a building shines through mist, dust or fume in the air. The 'dust lamp' reproduces this effect by producing a powerful parallel beam of light (see Figure 44). It shows the density and movement of particle clouds in its path. The user should move the lamp to illuminate different parts of the cloud and indicate the full cloud size and behaviour.[26] The competent LEV contractor has a dust lamp, and knows how to use it.

How to use a dust lamp

290 When using a dust lamp, do the following:

- Examine the work process. Where are the contaminant sources?
- Use the dust lamp on a tripod to light the potential source.
- Run the process.
- Stand off the axis of the light beam. Shielding your eyes from the lamp with an opaque barrier, look up the light beam. View the forward scattering of light from the particle cloud.

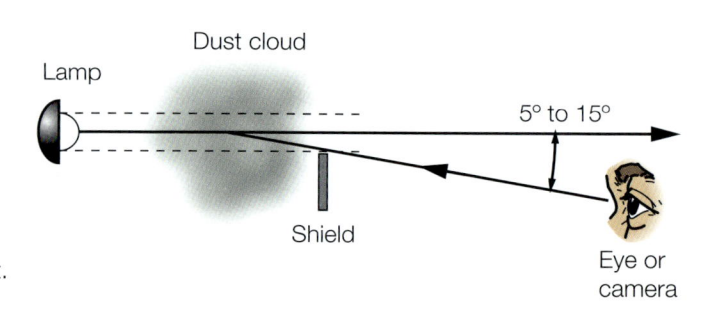

Figure 44 How to use a dust lamp

291 Also note:

- A tripod is essential for beam positioning.
- Rechargeable torches are available, suitable for use as a dust lamp.
- The dust lamp's parallel beam may only illuminate a part of the cloud.
- A dark background helps to reveal scattered light, eg a dark cloth.
- Turn out the workroom lights if you can, as long as this creates no safety risk.

Making air movement visible using smoke

292 Smoke from pellets, smoke tubes or smoke generators can:

- simulate the size, velocity and behaviour of dust clouds;
- identify capture zones and boundaries;
- confirm containment within a hood;
- identify draughts and air currents;
- determine the direction of general ventilation in a workroom.

293 The choice of smoke generator depends on the type and size of the source and hood:

- Smoke tubes produce a small amount of smoke as a single cloud. Some produce an acidic mist. They are often useful for testing smaller hoods.
- Smoke generators can produce variable amounts of smoke for prolonged periods. They use oil, propylene glycol etc that can leave residues. They are usually unsuitable where smoke detectors are fitted, unless

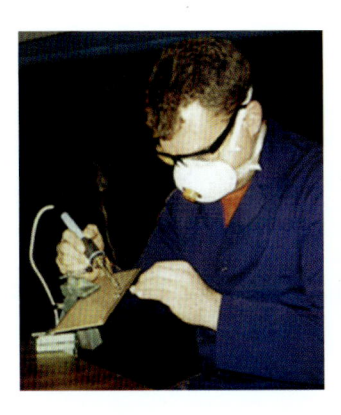

Figure 45 Soldering with and without Tyndall illumination

these can be isolated. Smoke generators have many uses, including assessing the effectiveness of large enclosing hoods.
- Smoke pellets produce a moderate amount of smoke for a short period. They are inappropriate with flammable substances nearby. They are useful for testing canopies and flues.

Quantitative assessment methods

294 Quantitative methods produce a reproducible measurement of performance. The test records are available for future comparison, as benchmarks. Methods include:

- measuring the flow rates at various points including hood faces and ducts, hood ducts and the main duct;
- measuring static pressures in various parts of the system including hood ducting and the pressure drop across filters and fans;
- the fan speed, motor speed and power consumption.

Instruments for testing

295 There is a need to calibrate measuring instruments. Use intrinsically safe instruments where there may be flammable atmospheres. The types of tests and equipment are:

- **Pressure testing**: Equipment includes manometers, Pitot tubes and micro-manometer or inclined manometer, velometers and pressure gauges.
- **Air velocity testing**: Equipment includes anemometers and velometers.
- **Testing control effectiveness**: Equipment includes spinning discs and tracer gases with a detector.
- **Fan testing**: Equipment includes tachometers and power consumption meters.
- **Filter or air cleaner performance testing**: Equipment includes isokinetic and size-selective sampling, water quality test kit.
- **Observation**: Dust lamp, smoke-generation equipment, camera, fibre-optic camera and boroscope.

Air sampling

296 Proof of effective control is the critical test, and air sampling may be appropriate. Sampling is carried out once all elements of the system are established, including correct operator behaviour. It generally requires a professional occupational hygienist, who makes:

- a careful choice of appropriate sampling methods;
- accurate measurements;
- a professional interpretation of the results.

297 Simple, off-the-shelf LEV and small LEV systems to control hazardous substances with lower toxicity can be tested, where feasible, with meters or detector tubes. Large or complex systems often require air sampling, particularly where the source is energetic. Air sampling means a combination of 'static samples' near the hood, personal sampling (operator and others) and emission sampling as appropriate.[27, 28]

Stage 4: Reports

298 Data on test points and design performance should also appear in the LEV user manual. The schedule for checks and maintenance should appear in the logbook.

LEV commissioning report

299 This is produced by the LEV commissioner and contains the key results of the LEV system commissioning. It provides a reference against which to compare regular checks and maintenance and statutory thorough examination and testing (see Chapter 10). The commissioning report confirms that the LEV system is performing as designed and that, in the commissioner's professional opinion, the system delivers adequate control of exposure.

300 The report must be clear, and show all relevant calculations. This enables volume flow rates, velocities and pressures to be compared with the design specification. Any mismatch shows a need to alter the LEV performance (eg change damper settings), to bring it back into specification. This is not necessarily simple. It may be that only diagnostic testing can identify the defect.

301 The commissioner should enter relevant information on performance, such as pressure and velocity results in the LEV user manual, and the benchmark findings of commissioning into the logbook for the system.

302 Where the effectiveness of the system depends on how it is used, the required procedures and practices need to be recorded in the user manual and the commissioning report.

Report contents

303 The report must contain:

- diagrams and a description of the LEV, including test points;
- details of the LEV performance specification;
- results, such as pressures and velocities at stated points;
- calculations;
- a written description of the commissioning, the qualitative and quantitative tests undertaken, and the outcome. Where necessary, this should include air sampling results;
- a description of operator behaviour for optimum LEV effectiveness.

304 An example of a suitable report form can be found on the HSE website: www.hse.gov.uk/lev.

Table 17 Principles of commissioning

Installation	Install according to the design specification. Check the layout and components against the plan. Agree any modifications with the designer/supplier. Check active parts of the system work (eg fan, air cleaner). Check a multi-branch system is (roughly) balanced. Record any variations. Include accessible cleaning and testing points.
Safe working procedures	Agree safe working procedures and responsibilities with the employer. Make sure any assessments and permits are in place, eg COSHH assessments and permits-to-work. Modify standard risk assessments covering on-site work.
Technical performance	Check the installation is correct and according to the design plan. The performance of hood, duct, air cleaner, air mover and discharge should all be correct. Make qualitative and quantitative checks. Balance a multi-branch system.
Control effectiveness	Verify the effectiveness of control. Check against installation and technical performance. Check operators are following correct ways of working. Make qualitative and quantitative checks to measure exposure control.
Commissioning report	Needs to be detailed enough. Agree this with the employer – this is part of the contract.
Transfer relevant data to the user manual and logbook	This is part of the contract. Documents should have space for relevant results and observations. Identify benchmarks and enter them in the logbook for the system.

9 User manual and logbook

Key point

- LEV system owners (employers) need both a 'user manual' and a system 'logbook'.

305 This chapter describes essential documentation for LEV systems.

Introduction

306 A user manual and logbook should be supplied as part of the design, installation and commissioning process. They contain standards for the thorough examination and test of LEV (see Chapter 10).

User manual

307 When buying virtually any machine, it comes with a user manual. LEV systems should be no different. A manual should cover how to use the system, how to maintain it, the spares available and a list of things that can go wrong. It should contain an exploded diagram naming key components of the LEV.

308 The employer, as client and owner of the LEV system, requires a user manual because:

- they may not understand the technicalities of the LEV system;
- LEV checking and maintenance will improve with good instructions and guidance;
- compliance with examination and test needs to improve.

309 A comprehensive user manual for LEV should be in two parts:

- simple 'getting started' instructions (to be read by most people); and
- detailed technical information for service providers and maintenance/repair engineers.

310 The detailed technical information should include:

- the purpose and description of the LEV system, including diagrams and drawings;
- how to use the LEV;
- signs of wear and control failure;
- the schedule, frequency and description of checks, maintenance and replacement;
- a detailed description of the specific statutory 'thorough examination and test' requirements and benchmarks;
- the performance information from commissioning;
- a listing of replaceable parts (and part numbers).

Purpose

311 There should be a description of what the LEV system is designed to control and how it achieves control.

Detailed description

312 The detailed description should include:

- Component specification and materials of construction and component serial numbers.
- The designed face velocities of all hoods and the duct velocities. Where the system components have 'type test' reports, these should be included.
- Make-up air arrangements.
- The measurement and test points, and the measurements and tests required. This includes testing alarms. For systems that use water, it includes tests of water quality. Where necessary, tests also include light levels at the work position.
- Maintenance and cleaning frequencies, eg fan blades, filters.
- Checks for articles blocking LEV.
- Correct operator behaviour in using the system, eg moveable hood positioning.
- Any special requirements for waste disposal.

Drawing

313 A drawing of the system should include identified components and, where appropriate, their serial numbers, showing:

- Hoods, including air inlets and if appropriate, their capture zone.
- Ductwork runs (rigid and flexible), bends and junctions, contractions and expansions.
- Control dampers and valves.
- Monitoring equipment, eg manometers.
- Measurement and test positions and (if necessary) sampling positions.
- Access hatches.
- Air cleaner (if fitted).
- Air mover.
- Discharge.
- Monitors and alarms.

Operation and use

314 The details of operation and use should include:

- Identification of adjustable controls that affect the system's performance, eg dampers, or using compressed air.
- The position of hoods, sash openings etc for optimum performance.
- Operator practice, including positioning of process equipment and methods of working. (This needs consultation with the employer and employees.)
- Hazards associated with the LEV system.

Checking and maintenance

315 The details of checking and maintenance should include:

- Ductwork condition, especially flexible ducts.
- Mechanical integrity, eg corrosion, damage, seals, dampers, sash suspensions etc.
- Cleanliness of hoods, especially canopies and duct interiors.
- Operation of monitors, flow indicators etc.
- Pressure relief or inerting systems, if applicable.
- Test for leakage.
- Illumination in booths and hoods.
- Noise levels.
- Alarm systems operate correctly.
- Water quality if appropriate.
- Make-up air without draughts or blockages.
- List of spare parts required.

Thorough examination and testing

316 The details of thorough examination and testing should include:

- What to test.
- When to test.
- Where to test.
- How to test.
- Comparison with commissioning and subsequent test results.
- Commissioning report.

Technical performance

317 The details of technical performance should include:

- Static pressure target values for each hood, duct, and other identified points in the system.
- Target hood face velocity and other velocities.
- The operators' (employees') exposure compared with exposure benchmarks.

LEV system logbook

318 All LEV systems require a logbook that contains schedules and forms to keep records of regular checking, maintenance and repair. The logbook contains:

- Schedules for regular checks and maintenance.
- Records of regular checks, maintenance, replacements and repairs.
- Checks of compliance with the correct way of working with the LEV system.
- The name of the person who made these checks.

Examples of what should appear in the logbook's checklists

319 Identified daily checks, weekly checks and monthly checks for each item in the system, for example:

- Hoods, including static pressure (manometer indication), physical damage and blockages.
- Ducts, including damage, wear and partial blockage.
- Dampers – position.
- Air cleaner, including damage, static pressure across the cleaner, and failure alarms.
- Air mover, including power consumption and changes in noise or vibration.
- Maintenance carried out.
- Replacements made.
- Planned and unplanned repairs.
- Operator's use of the LEV – check they are following correct procedures.
- Space to report the results against each check item.
- Signature and date.

320 Specific examples include:

- Clearance time for a room enclosure or booth.
- Receiving hood positioning, particularly for moveable hoods.
- Capturing hood and working zone within the capture zone.
- Operator avoidance of plumes of rising hot contaminant clouds.

- Operator making sure the source is well within a partial enclosure.
- Operator working sideways-on to the airflow in a walk-in booth.
- Clutter obstructing LEV.
- Checking the fan noise and keeping the impellers clean.
- Fan bearing replacement.
- Filter material replacement.

Undocumented existing systems

321 For LEV systems with no logbook, user manual or commissioning report, the employer needs help from the supplier or from an expert, eg a consultant engineer or occupational hygienist.

322 Qualitative methods to check effectiveness are adequate where a simple LEV system appears to be effective. In all other cases, quantitative methods are needed, eg measured pressure and airflow data, recorded to act as benchmarks in a new logbook. But where the LEV is ineffective, the employer should engage an LEV supplier or designer for help.

10 Thorough examination and test

Key points

- Every employer's LEV system requires statutory 'thorough examination and testing' by a competent person.
- The examination and testing report must have a prioritised list of any remedial actions for the employer.
- The employer's engineer and person responsible for health and safety both need to see the report.

323 This chapter describes the statutory examination and test required for LEV systems.

Introduction

324 Routine checks (daily, weekly, and monthly) keep the LEV system running properly. The frequency of routine checks and their description should be set out in the system logbook. A trained employee is able to make routine checks. Employees should report any defects in LEV to their supervisor. The employer must ensure that those who check or examine LEV have adequate knowledge, training and expertise.

325 The thorough examination and test serves as an audit of the past year's LEV system management. The objective of testing is to find significant defects and to have them remedied to regain control. The items for statutory examination and test should be set out in the user manual and the expertise of a service provider may be needed.

326 The COSHH Regulations require thorough maintenance, examination and test of control measures at intervals so that controls remain effective at all times. 'Controls' mean more than just the 'hardware' and include:

- the LEV;
- parts that deteriorate, eg valves, seals, connections; and
- employees following correct ways of working.

Thorough examination and test

327 'Thorough' means careful, methodical, painstaking and complete. The thorough examination and test may be carried out by:

- an outside contractor; or
- a competent employee of the LEV owner (the employer).

328 Information on the 'competence' of the LEV examiner appears in Chapter 2 and Appendix 1.

Frequency of thorough examination and test

329 The maximum time between tests of LEV systems is set down in COSHH and for most systems this is 14 months (see the exceptions in Table 18). In practice this is normally taken to mean annually. If wear and tear on the LEV system is liable to mean that the system effectiveness will degrade between tests then thorough examinations and tests should be more frequent.

Table 18 Legal maximum intervals for thorough examination and test of LEV plant used in certain processes

Process	Minimum frequency
Processes in which blasting is carried out in or incidental to the cleaning of metal castings in connection with their manufacture	1 month
Jute cloth manufacture	1 month
Processes, other than wet processes, in which metals (other than gold, platinum or iridium) are ground, abraded or polished using mechanical power, in any room for more than 12 hours a week	6 months
Processes giving off dust or fume in which non-ferrous metal castings are produced	6 months

330 In practice, some of these intervals may be helpful in suggesting suitable reduced intervals for testing of similar processes, eg abrasive blasting of articles other than castings: 1 month.

331 There should be regular audits of administrative procedures (eg following checking schedules) and behavioural controls (including supervision).

Preparing to check, maintain, repair and examine LEV

332 The LEV examiner needs to know the risks from the system under test. These include:

- health risks from residues within the systems;
- safety risks from mechanical parts of the LEV, work at height, electricity, manual handling and moving vehicles.

333 The employer and examiner need to co-operate to ensure minimal risk for both service provider and employees (operators) who may be affected by the work. The employer should arrange for permits-to-work (where necessary) and space for access. The employer should also provide information about personal protective equipment requirements.

334 For statutory thorough examination and test, the examiner should, where available, use the following information sources:

- the LEV system commissioning report;
- the LEV user manual;
- the logbook for the system;
- the previous LEV system statutory report;
- confirmation that there have been no changes to the LEV, layout or process since the last test.

335 The examiner should verify that the documents apply to the system under test. If none of these documents is available, an adequate 'thorough examination and test' would take the status of a commissioning report. In such cases, the examiner's report must contain sufficient detail to produce (and may actually include) a logbook for the system.

Carrying out a thorough examination and test

336 The examination and test procedure and methods are similar to the original commissioning exercise, with similar visual testing and measurement methods. Thorough examination and testing of LEV involves three stages:

Stage 1 A thorough visual examination to verify the LEV is in efficient working order, in good repair and in a clean condition.
Stage 2 Measuring and examining the technical performance to check conformity with commissioning data.
Stage 3 Assessment to check the control of worker exposure is adequate.

337 System examiners need equipment such as Pitot tubes, a smoke generator, a dust lamp, an anemometer and, sometimes, equipment for air sampling.

Stage 1 Thorough visual and structural examination

338 This may include, as appropriate:

- thorough external examination of all parts of the system for damage, wear and tear;
- internal duct and hatch seal examinations;
- checks that any filter cleaning devices (shake-down, reverse or pulsed jet) work correctly;
- inspection of the filter fabric. Where filters have built-in pressure gauges, checks on their function (and that the operating pressure is correct);
- checks of the water flow and sump condition in a wet scrubber;
- checks that monitors and alerts/alarms, eg for returned air, are functioning;
- inspection of the air mover drive mechanism, eg fan belt;
- checks for indications of effectiveness. Are there significant deposits of settled dust in and around the LEV hood? Is any part of the system vibrating or noisy?

Stage 2 Measure technical performance

339 This may include, as appropriate:

- measuring the air velocities at suitable test points indicated in the system documentation. This includes hood faces, branch ducts and the main duct;
- measuring static pressure at suitable test points indicated in the system documentation. This includes all hoods, ducting, across the air cleaner and fan;
- checking the fan speed, motor speed and electrical power consumption;
- checking the replacement or make-up air supply;
- testing alarms, by simulating a failure, and the alarm's ability to detect the failure;
- measuring air temperatures;
- testing the air cleaner performance (eg a recirculating system).

340 Environmental legislation may require testing of air discharges but this is not covered by this book (see www.netregs.gov.uk).

341 The examiner should calculate volume flow rates. The next steps are:

- to compare the results of testing with the LEV design specification as reported in system documentation such as the user manual and the system logbook;
- to diagnose the causes of discrepancies. With the employer's consent, the examiner may make simple alterations that restore the required performance. An example is where displaced dampers cause a multi-branch system to be out-of-balance; the examiner may re-balance the system.

342 If the defect is fundamental or obscure, the examination should stop until the system has been repaired and its original performance restored. The examiner should warn the client promptly.

Stage 3 Assess control effectiveness

343 This may include, as appropriate:

- careful observation of processes and sources;
- assessment of how effective the LEV is at controlling operators' exposure;
- challenge tests with smoke with the process running, to check for smoke leakage, eddying and breathing zone encroachment. (When smoke testing, the examiner should warn employees and may need smoke alarms turned off);
- dust lamp tests with the process running to check for escape of dust or mist;
- observation of the way operators work, whether they are using the methods specified and whether these methods are sustainable.

Marking hoods

344 The examiner should attach a test label to each hood when tested (see Figure 46). Where control failure requires remedy or repair, the examiner should instead attach a red 'fail' label to the hood (see Figure 47).

345 Employees who use the LEV system and their supervisors need this testing information. All hoods should carry a test label.

Test record:

Test date:............................	
Next test:............................	
Examiner:............................	

Figure 46 A test label for an LEV hood

Inadequate control:

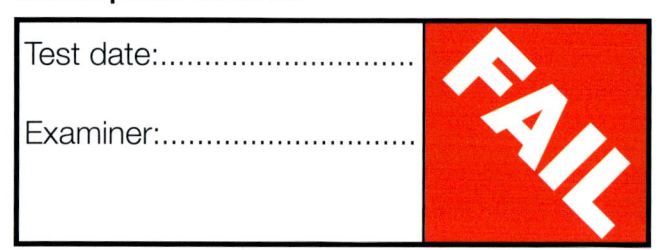

| Test date:............................ | FAIL |
| Examiner:............................ | |

Figure 47 A fail label for an LEV hood

346 The criteria for a red label are:

- No airflow.
- Failure of an enclosing hood to contain the contaminant cloud.
- Failure of a receiving hood to intercept or contain the contaminant cloud.
- Failure of a capturing hood, eg the capture zone does not encompass the working zone.

347 It may be useful to use a red label for other parts of the LEV system that have clearly failed.

Report of LEV thorough examination and test

348 The HSE website (www.hse.gov.uk/lev) has a form for recording this information. The examiner judges whether the system is effectively controlling exposure to substance(s) hazardous to health and produces a prioritised plan for any actions. The employer should understand what actions are required, and if these are uncertain, contact an LEV supplier for expert help. Where maintenance or repairs are identified as priorities for action, the employer should plan and schedule such repair, and re-test to assure control.

349 The information in the report must include:

- the name and address of the employer responsible for the LEV;
- the date of examination and test;
- the date of the last thorough examination and test;
- the identification and location of the LEV, and the process and hazardous substance concerned;
- the conditions at the time of the test and whether this was normal production or special conditions;
- a simple diagram of the LEV layout and location, with test points;
- the condition of the LEV system including hood serial numbers and photographs of relevant parts;
- its intended operating performance for adequately controlling the hazardous substance and whether it is still achieving the same performance;
- the methods used to make a judgement of performance and what needs to be done to achieve that performance, eg visual, pressure measurements, airflow measurements, dust lamp, air sampling, tests to check the condition and effectiveness of the filter;
- the results of any air sampling relevant to LEV performance;
- comments on the way operators used the LEV;
- comments on system wear and tear and whether components may need repair or replacement before the next annual test;
- the name, job title and employer of the person carrying out the examination and test;
- the signature of the person carrying out the examination and test;
- the details of any minor adjustments or repairs carried out to make the LEV system effective. Note: The employer needs to know about critical defects immediately and should not wait for the report.

350 The employer should keep the examination and test report for at least five years. A copy should be available at the workplace containing the LEV system.

351 Where the LEV system was previously undocumented, the record should be a suitable basis for a system logbook.

Specific LEV measurements

352 These measurements are additional to qualitative tests – observation, smoke and dust lamp.

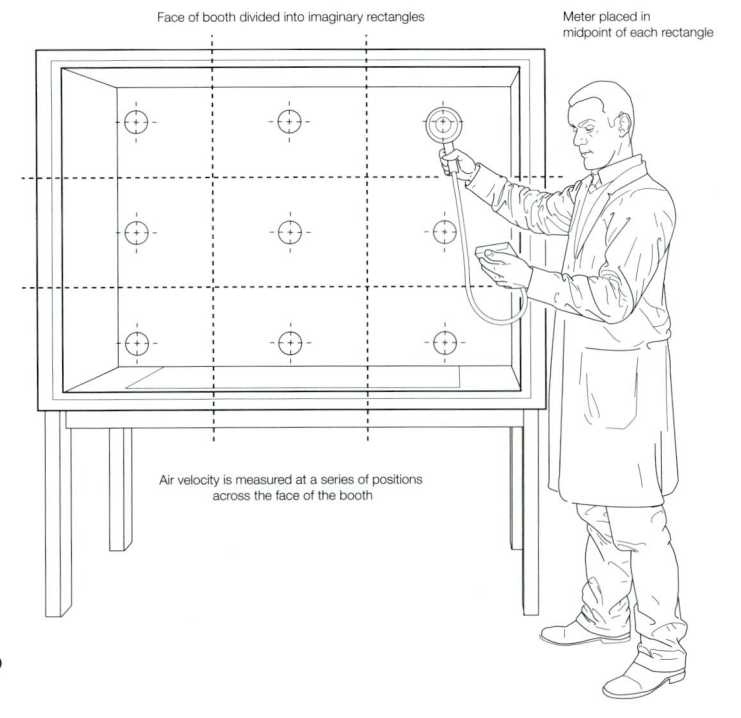

Figure 48 Testing large hood face velocities

Full enclosures

353 Measure the static pressure between the interior of the enclosure and the workroom. The pressure in the interior must be lower than the workroom.

Partial enclosures – Booths/fume cupboards

354 Measure the face velocity (see Figure 48). No reading should vary by more than 20% from the average. Fume cupboards and microbiological safety cabinets should also be further tested according to appropriate BS or EN Standards.

Receiving hoods including canopies and capturing hoods

355 Measure the face velocity. For larger hoods, measure at several points over the face. No reading should vary by more than 20% from the average.

Capturing hoods – Slots

356 Measure the air velocities at equidistant points along the entire length and average the readings. No reading should vary by more than 20% from the average.

Hood ducts

357 Check the manometer static pressure reading. Check that the reading is correct. If there is no manometer fitted, record the need to fit one in the 'action plan'.

Plenums

358 Measure the static pressure of the plenum (the enclosure behind certain types of hood) as well as the hood duct measurement.

Ducts

359 Measure the air velocity in the duct serving each hood, where this is possible. Measure in a straight section of duct – the measuring point should be well downstream of bends and other turbulence sources.

Fan/air mover

360 Measure the static pressure at the fan inlet and the volume flow rate. Measure the volume flow rate either on the fan inlet or outlet, wherever there is a reasonably straight section of duct – the measuring point should be well downstream of bends and other turbulence. For a belt-driven fan, measure the rate of revolution of the fan shaft with a tachometer.

Filters

361 Measure the static pressure across the filter. Where a fabric filter has a shake-down cleaning device, operate the shake-down before taking measurements. If the air volume passing through the filter is the same as that through the fan, the filter flow rate need not be measured.

362 Measure the accuracy of any fitted pressure gauges.

Special filter

363 Filtration of 'toxic' particles requires a high performance filter – high efficiency particle arrestors ('HEPA' or 'absolute' filters) are used. Follow an appropriate British, European or ISO standard to test such filters *in situ*.

Wet scrubber

364 Measure the static pressure at the inlet and outlet, and the water pH if relevant to the scrubbing performance.

Appendix 1 Legal requirements

1 This appendix summarises the legal duties placed on those concerned with LEV (including manufacture, supply, commissioning, use, maintenance, testing etc). For more details, look at relevant HSE publications.[3, 4, 6] It does not cover legal matters relating to flammability (DSEAR) or environmental legislation.

Who has responsibilities?

2 Health and safety law is aimed mainly at employers and the self-employed and, to a lesser degree, employees and others. The responsibilities of the self-employed, with regard to LEV systems, are the same as for employers and, for brevity, the use of the term 'employer' in this guidance also includes the self-employed.

3 Under the Health and Safety at Work etc Act 1974 (the HSW Act), every employer has health and safety duties to themselves, their employees, and other people who may be affected by the way they carry out their work ('conduct their undertaking'). It is important to remember that companies who sell LEV or provide related services are also employers conducting an undertaking. This means that anyone who, for example, supplies, installs, commissions or tests LEV, has health and safety duties with respect to the people who use it (or are meant to be protected by it). Consequently, it is not just the owner of an LEV system who has responsibilities.

4 The HSW Act also takes account of offences which are primarily the fault of other people. For example, a client company may have employed the services of what they could justly assume was a competent person (see Chapter 2 and paragraphs 11-16 of this appendix for information on competence) to assess health risks, commission LEV etc. If the actions (or following the advice) of the competent person exposes the client's employees to a health risk, this could leave the client in breach of the law. Under the HSW Act, however, the competent person could be charged with the offence (irrespective of whether the proceedings are taken against the client) because the competent person was the real cause of the breach being committed.

5 The Control of Substances Hazardous to Health (COSHH) Regulations 2002 (as amended) add specific requirements to the generality of the HSW Act. For example:

- Employers must assess the degree of exposure and the risks to their employees, devise and implement adequate control measures, and check and maintain them.
- Employees must use these control measures in the way they are intended to be used and as they have been instructed.
- Employers must ensure that the equipment necessary for control is maintained 'in an efficient state, in efficient working order, in good repair and in a clean condition'.
- Employers must ensure that thorough examination and testing of their 'protective'* LEV is carried out every 14 months (unless otherwise stipulated), other engineering controls at 'suitable intervals' and must 'review and revise' ways of working so that controls are being used effectively.
- The frequency of examination and tests should be linked to the type of engineering control in use, the size of the risk if it failed or deteriorated and how likely it is to fail or deteriorate.
- Employers and employees should give the person carrying out the thorough examination and test all the co-operation needed for the work to be carried out correctly and fully.
- Any defects should be put right as soon as possible or within a time laid down by the person who carries out the examination.
- The person carrying out the thorough examination and test should provide a record, which needs to be kept by the employer for at least 5 years (see Chapter 10 for what this should include).

Safety of machinery

6 Machinery is required to be safe and without risks to health with respect to the way it performs, eg there should be no accessible dangerous parts. Suppliers also need to provide sufficient information to users to ensure this can be achieved. Machines may also create hazardous emissions related to the materials that they work on, for example, wood dust or metalworking fluid mist.

7 The Supply of Machinery (Safety) Regulations (SMSR)[29] apply to machinery that was first provided for use in the European Economic Area after 1 January 1993. From an LEV perspective, this includes:

- emission generators, such as machines for turning, grinding and drilling that emit dust, and lathes that emit metalworking fluid mist;

---

* LEV may have been required for reasons other than COSHH, eg nuisance.

- emission controllers, such as LEV hoods, and moveable extraction equipment, as long as these fall within the 'machinery' definition;
- general equipment associated with a need for dust control where an activity creates the contaminant cloud, such as bag weighing at a bag filling station.

8 SMSR implement the Machinery Directive (98/37/EC[30]). 'Machines' (as defined by the Directive) must meet 'essential health and safety requirements' (EHSRs). This includes being capable of containing or extracting the contaminant cloud. The machine designer, manufacturer and supplier have the duty to comply with this EHSR.[31, 32] But in the case of 'general equipment', their duties are limited by their knowledge of the process, with no requirement to design any LEV provision if they do not know the nature of the hazardous substance.

9 The machine supplier might not supply the LEV components, but may specify an extraction rate. The machine owner is then responsible for ensuring extraction is adequate to control exposure.

10 EN standards apply to machinery. Where the SMSR and EN standards do not apply, eg certain cases of 'general equipment', section 6 of the HSW Act will still apply and the supplier is required to ensure that the equipment is safe to use as intended.

Competence

11 Competence means having appropriate knowledge, capabilities and experience. This will include, for instance, anyone who:

- designs or selects control measures;
- checks, tests and maintains control measures;
- supplies goods and services to employers for health and safety purposes.

12 The Management of Health and Safety at Work Regulations 1999 (MHSWR) state that:

- An employer should be competent for health and safety purposes or employ or obtain advice from competent people.
- People are seen as competent where they have enough training and experience or knowledge and other qualities to enable them 'properly to assist in undertaking the measures referred to'.

13 Simple situations may require only:

- an understanding of relevant best practice;
- an awareness of the limitations of one's own experience and knowledge; and
- the willingness and ability to supplement existing experience.

14 More complicated situations will require the competent assistant to have a higher level of knowledge and experience. Employers are advised to check the appropriate health and safety qualifications.

15 The COSHH Regulations require that:

- employers ensure any person (whether or not their employee) who carries out work in connection with the employer's duties under the COSHH Regulations has suitable and sufficient information, instruction and training;
- employers ensure whoever provides advice on the prevention or control of exposure is competent to do so;
- whoever designs control measures needs appropriate knowledge, skills and experience;
- anyone who checks on the effectiveness of any element of a control measure should be competent to do so.

LEV competence: Design, supply, commission and test of LEV systems

16 General engineering courses do not confer competence in effective LEV design, application and thorough examination and test. Relatively few businesses and consultants specialise in LEV. Routes to becoming professionally competent include qualifications through BOHS, UKAS and CIBSE (see Chapter 2 and 'Useful contacts'). Checklists for competence appear in Chapter 2.

Appendix 2 Selecting a 'control benchmark' and 'control requirement'

1   This appendix describes a series of steps with worked examples to show how to assess a benchmark for the specification of LEV:

Step 1   Select the hazard band.
Step 2   Identify the exposure benchmark.
Step 3   Look at the 'exposure matrix'.

Step 1 Select the hazard band

2   There are five hazard bands, A to E. A is the least hazardous and E is the most hazardous (see Step 2).

Hazard band	Hazard classification	
	CHIP* R-phrase numbers	GHS** H-phrase numbers
A	36, 38, 65, 67 and all not otherwise listed	303, 304, 305, 313, 315, 316, 318, 319, 320, 333, 336 and all not otherwise listed
B	20, 21, 22, 68/20/21/22	302, 312, 332, 371
C	23, 24, 25, 34, 35, 37, 41, 43, 48/20/21/22, 39/23/24/25, 68/23/24/25	301, 311, 314, 317, 318, 331, 335, 370, 373
D	26, 27, 28, 40, 60, 61, 62, 63, 64, 48/23/24/25, 39/26/27/28	300, 310, 330, 351, 360, 361, 362, 372
E	42, 45, 46, 49, 68	334, 340, 341, 350

* Chemicals (Hazard Information and Packaging for Supply) Regulations 2002 (as amended) (CHIP) – Risk 'R' phrase
** Globally Harmonised System (GHS) – Hazard 'H' phrase: interim hazard banding

Example
You need to use the highest band in which any of the 'R' phrase numbers appear. A product classified as R20 R36/37/38 R65 is hazard band C, because R37 is in Band C. A product classified as R68/21/22 R43 is also hazard Band C. A product classified as R20/21/22 R68 is hazard band E.

Step 2 Identify the exposure benchmark

Hazard of emitted material Band A to E (COSHH essentials)	Exposure benchmark range	
	Dust/mist	Vapour/gas
A: Unclassified as harmful	1 to 10 mg/m^3	50 to 500 ppm
B: Harmful	0.1 to 1 mg/m^3	5 to 50 ppm
C: Toxic, corrosive	0.01 to 0.1 mg/m^3	0.5 to 5 ppm
D: Very toxic, toxic to reproduction	less than 0.01 mg/m^3	less than 0.5 ppm
E: Carcinogen, mutagen, asthmagen	'As low as is reasonably practicable'	

3   The benchmark should be the lower value in the exposure benchmark range.

Example
A product classified as hazard band C is associated with an exposure benchmark range between 0.01 to 0.1 mg/m^3 (dust/mist) or 0.5 to 5 ppm (vapour/gas). The benchmark is either 0.01 mg/m^3 (dust/mist) or 0.5 ppm (vapour/gas).

Control specification

4   The technical basis for 'COSHH essentials' (www.coshh-essentials.org.uk/assets/live/cetb.pdf) can identify a control solution. It uses an 'exposure matrix' that associates liquid volatility or dustiness with a typical exposure range and amount, assuming no controls are in place.

Liquid volatility

5   Boiling point or vapour pressure is the basis for selecting volatility:

- Low volatility liquids – vapour pressure less than 500 Pa.
- Medium volatility liquids – vapour pressure between 500 and 25 000 Pa.
- High volatility liquids – vapour pressure above 25 000 Pa.

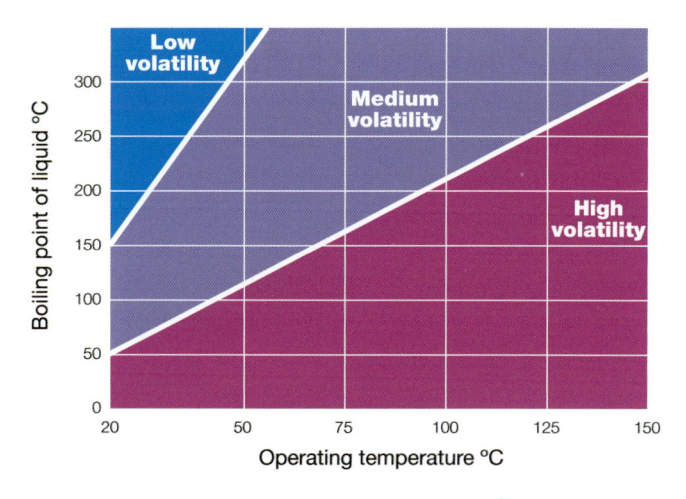

Figure 49 Graph to select volatility of liquid

6   Or select the volatility from the boiling point and process temperature (see Figure 49).

Solid dustiness

7   Judgement is the basis for selecting dustiness:

- Low dustiness solids – pellets and non-dusty solids.
- Medium dustiness solids – granules and coarse dusts.
- High dustiness solids – fine powders and solids that produce fine dust.

Amount

8   The amount is worked out as follows:

- **S**: Small amount – ml up to 1 litre (liquid); g up to 1 kg (solid).
- **M**: Medium amount – 1 litre up to 1000 litres (liquid); 1 kg up to 1000 kg (solid).
- **L**: Large amount – 1000 litres and above (liquid); 1 tonne and above (solid).

Step 3 'Exposure matrix'

	Liquid - Volatility		
ppm	Low	Medium	High
> 500			L
50 to 500		M, L	M
5 to 50	M, L	S	S
< 5	S		

	Solid - Dustiness		
mg/m³	Low	Medium	High
< 10		L	L
1 to 10		M	M
0.1 to 1	M, L		S
0.01 to 0.1	S	S	

Examples

A medium amount of a low volatility liquid is associated with an exposure range between 5 and 50 ppm.
A small amount of a high dustiness solid is associated with an exposure range between 0.1 and 1 mg/m³.

9   Recent research suggests that for sprayed liquids, the vapour concentrations in the matrix should be:

	Sprayed liquid - Volatility		
ppm	Low	Medium	High
> 500		M, L	M, L
50 to 500	M, L		
5 to 50		S	S
< 5	S		

10   The predicted exposure is the higher value in the exposure range (from Step 3). The control specification is derived from comparing a known or predicted exposure with the exposure benchmark (from Step 2).

Example: Known exposure limit and exposure

Rosin-core solder fume can cause asthma. It has a Workplace Exposure Limit (WEL) at 0.05 mg/m³ (8-hour TWA) and exposure must be reduced as far as is reasonably practicable below this limit, eg 0.01 mg/m³. Several mg/m³ of fume have been measured in solder fume smoke plumes. Given that solderers are close to the workpiece and that hot fume rises into the breathing zone, there is a need for LEV that reduces exposure one hundred-fold, ie Fume at 1 mg/m³ reduced to 0.01 mg/m³ = 100-fold reduction.

Example: Unknown exposure limit and exposure

5 kg of a liquid toxic product is in hazard band C (Steps 1 and 2), associated with an exposure benchmark range at 0.5 to 5 ppm. With a boiling point at 270°C and a process temperature at 130°C: the product has medium volatility (Figure 49). Step 3 shows 'liquid – medium amount – medium volatility' associated with exposures between 50 and 500 ppm. There is a need for LEV that reduces exposure one thousand-fold, ie Vapour at 500 ppm reduced to 0.5 ppm = 1000-fold reduction.

References

1 *COSHH a brief guide to the Regulations: What you need to know about the Control of Substances Hazardous to Health Regulations 2002 (COSHH)* Leaflet INDG136(rev3) HSE Books 2005 www.hse.gov.uk/pubns/indg136.pdf (A revised COSHH leaflet will replace this version in 2008)

2 *Clearing the air: A simple guide to buying and using local exhaust ventilation (LEV)* Leaflet INDG408 HSE Books 2008 (single copy free or priced packs of 15 ISBN 978 0 7176 6301 9) www.hse.gov.uk/pubns/indg408.pdf

3 *Control of substances hazardous to health (Fifth edition). The Control of Substances Hazardous to Health Regulations 2002 (as amended). Approved Code of Practice and guidance* L5 (Fifth edition) HSE Books 2005 ISBN 978 0 7176 2981 7

4 *Management of health and safety at work. Management of Health and Safety at Work Regulations 1999. Approved Code of Practice and guidance* L21 (Second edition) HSE Books 2000 ISBN 978 0 7176 2488 1

5 **R**egistration, **E**valuation, **A**uthorisation and restriction of **CH**emicals (REACH) www.hse.gov.uk/reach/index.htm

6 Supply of Machinery (Safety) Regulations 1992 (as amended) *Product standards – Machinery – A guide to the UK Regulations* URN 95/650 (May 1995) www.berr.gov.uk/files/file11274.pdf. Also see: www.berr.gov.uk/dius/innovation/regulations/ecdirect/ipsg/index.html

7 *Managing health and safety in construction. Construction (Design and Management) Regulations 2008. Approved Code of Practice* L144 HSE Books 2007 ISBN 978 0 7176 6223 4

8 *General methods for sampling and gravimetric analysis of respirable and inhalable dust* MDHS14/3 (Third edition) HSE Books 2000 www.hse.gov.uk/pubns/mdhs/index.htm

9 *Explosive atmospheres: Classification of hazardous areas (zoning) and selection of equipment* HSE online guidance www.hse.gov.uk/fireandexplosion/zoning.pdf

10 *Sizing of explosion relief vents* SHAPA Technical Bulletin No.10 (2004) www.shapa.co.uk/pdf/techdata10.pdf

11 *A summary of the technical basis for COSHH essentials* HSE 2003 www.coshh-essentials.org.uk/assets/live/cetb.pdf

12 *COSHH essentials: Easy steps to control health risks from chemicals* www.coshh-essentials.org.uk

13 *Industrial ventilation: A manual of recommended practice for design* (26th edition) ACGIH 2007 ISBN 978 1 882417 71 1 www.acgih.org

14 *CHIP for everyone* HSG228 HSE Books 2002 ISBN 978 0 7176 2370 9

15 *Ductwork (Heating, air conditioning and refrigeration)* CIBSE Guide B3 2002 ISBN 978 1 903287 20 0

16 *The Building Regulations 2000. Approved Document B. Fire safety* 2006 edition (amended 2007) www.planningportal.gov.uk/england/professionals/en/1115314110382.html

17 *Fire engineering (Fire safety)* CIBSE Guide E 2003 ISBN 978 1 903287 31 6

18 *Specification for sheet metal ductwork. Low, medium and high pressure/velocity air systems* DW/144 HVCA 1998 ISBN 978 0 903783 27 9

19 *Specification for plastics ductwork* DW/154 HVCA 2000 ISBN 978 0 903783 31 6

20 *Code of practice for resin-bonded glass fibre ductwork metric* DW/191 HVCA 1973

21 *Reference data (Heating, air conditioning and refrigeration)* CIBSE Guide C 2007 ISBN 978 1 9032 87 80 4

22 *Fan application guide (Ventilation and indoor air quality)* CIBSE 2006 ISBN 978 1 903287 68 2

23 BS EN 14175-2:2003 *Fume cupboards. Safety and performance requirements* British Standards Institution

24 *Commissioning air systems. Application procedures for buildings* (Third edition) BSRIA 2001 ISBN 978 0 86022 591 1

25 *Practices for measurement, testing, adjusting and balancing of building heating, ventilation, air-conditioning and refrigeration systems* Standard 111-1988 American Society of Heating, Refrigerating and Air-Conditioning Engineers (ASHRAE) 1988 ISBN/ISSN 1041-2336

26 *The dust lamp: A simple tool for observing the presence of airborne particles* MDHS82 HSE Books 1997 www.hse.gov.uk/pubns/mdhs/index.htm

27 *General methods for sampling airborne gases and vapours* MDHS70 HSE Books 1990 www.hse.gov.uk/pubns/mdhs/index.htm

28 *Exposure measurement: Air sampling* COSHH essentials sheet G409 HSE 2006 www.hse.gov.uk/pubns/guidance/g409.pdf

29 The Supply of Machinery (Safety) Regulations 1992 (www.opsi.gov.uk/SI/si1992/Uksi_19923073_en_1.htm), as amended by the Supply of Machinery (Safety) (Amendment) Regulations 1994 (www.opsi.gov.uk/SI/si1994/Uksi_19942063_en_1.htm)

30 Machinery Directive 89/392/EEC, amended 98/37/EC www.hse.gov.uk/aboutus/europe/euronews/july07/machinery.htm Also see http://ec.europa.eu/enterprise/newapproach/standardization/harmstds/reflist/machines.html

31 *Supplying new machinery: A short guide to the law and some information on what to do for anyone supplying machinery for use at work* Leaflet INDG270 HSE Books 1998 (single copy free or priced packs of 15 ISBN 978 0 7176 1560 5) www.hse.gov.uk/pubns/indg270.htm

32 *Buying new machinery: A short guide to the law and some information on what to do for anyone buying new machinery for use at work* Leaflet INDG271 HSE Books 1998 (single copy free or priced packs of 15 ISBN 978 0 7176 1559 9) www.hse.gov.uk/pubns/indg271.htm

Further reading

A guide to energy efficient ventilation Martin Liddament AIVC 1996 ISBN 0 946075 85 9

Companion study guide to industrial ventilation: A manual of recommended practice for design (26th Edition) D Jeff Burton ACGIH 2007 ISBN 978 1 882417 76 6 www.acgih.org

Fan and ductwork installation guide First edition HEVAC www.feta.co.uk/downloads/listing.pdf Available from FETA, 2 Waltham Court, Milley Lane, Hare Hatch, Reading, Berkshire RG10 9TH

Handbook of ventilation for contaminant control Third edition Henry J McDermott 2001 ISBN 978 1 882417 38 4

Hemeon WCL *Plant and process ventilation* 3rd edition Lewis 1998 Edited D Jeff Burton ISBN 978 1 56670 347 5

Indoor air quality case studies reference guide George J Benda Editor Fairmont Press 1998 ISBN 978 0 88173 305 1

Principles of good control practice www.bohs.org >publications > guidance > COSHH Good Control Practice Summary and Check List

ANSI/AIHA standards

Exhaust systems for grinding, polishing, and buffing ANSI/AIHA Z9.6-1999 ISBN 978 0 932627 95 7 www.aiha.org

Fundamentals governing the design and operation of dilution ventilation systems in industrial occupancies ANSI/AIHA Z9.10-2007 ISBN 978 1 931504 86 7 www.aiha.org

Fundamentals governing the design and operation of local exhaust ventilation systems ANSI/AIHA Z9.2-2006 ISBN 978 1 931504 73 7 www.aiha.org

Laboratory ventilation ANSI/AIHA Z9.5-2003 ISBN 978 1 931504 35 5 www.aiha.org

Recirculation of air from industrial process exhaust systems ANSI/AIHA Z9.7-2007 ISBN 978 1 931504 79 9 www.aiha.org

Spray finishing operations: Safety code for design, construction, and ventilation ANSI/AIHA Z9.3-2007 ISBN 978 1 931504 85 0 www.aiha.org

Ventilation and control of airborne contaminants during open-surface tank operations ANSI/AIHA Z9.1-2006 ISBN 978 1 931504 72 0 www.aiha.org

HSE publications

Controlling exposure to stonemasonry dust: Guidance for employers HSG201 HSE Books 2001 ISBN 978 0 7176 1760 9

EH40/2005 Workplace exposure limits: Containing the list of workplace exposure limits for use with the Control of Substances Hazardous to Health Regulations 2002 (as amended) Environmental Hygiene Guidance Note EH40 HSE Books 2005 ISBN 978 0 7176 2977 0 (Also see list of workplace exposure limits at www.hse.gov.uk/coshh/table1.pdf.)

Evaluation of commercial spot lamps for use as dust lamps RR631 (This report will be published in mid-2008 and will be available at www.hse.gov.uk/research/rrhtm/rr631.htm)

Fire and explosion: How safe is your workplace? A short guide to the Dangerous Substances and Explosive Atmospheres Regulations Leaflet INDG370 HSE Books 2002 (single copy free or priced packs of 5 ISBN 978 0 7176 2589 5) www.hse.gov.uk/pubns/indg370.pdf

Safe work in confined spaces Leaflet INDG258 HSE Books 1997 (single copy free or priced packs of 20 ISBN 978 0 7176 1442 4) www.hse.gov.uk/pubns/indg258.pdf

Safe working with flammable substances Leaflet INDG227 HSE Books 1996 (single copy free or priced packs of 15 ISBN 978 0 7176 1154 6) www.hse.gov.uk/pubns/indg227.pdf

Time to clear the air!: A workers' pocket guide to local exhaust ventilation (LEV) Pocket card INDG409 HSE Books 2008 (single copy free or priced packs of 25 ISBN 978 0 7176 6300 2) www.hse.gov.uk/pubns/indg409.pdf

This book (HSG258) is also available to buy as a pack with a DVD *Everybody needs to breathe* HSE Books ISBN 978 0 7176 6304 0

Useful contacts

American Conference of Governmental Industrial Hygienists (ACGIH) www.acgih.org
American member-based organisation for occupational and environmental health, with many publications.

American National Standards Institute (ANSI)
www.ansi.org
Actionable information on national, regional, international standards and conformity assessment issues.

American Society of Heating, Refrigerating and Air-Conditioning Engineers (ASHRAE) www.ashrae.org
International technical society of heating, ventilation, air-conditioning and refrigeration.

British Occupational Hygiene Society (BOHS),
5/6 Melbourne Business Court, Millennium Way, Pride Park, Derby DE24 8LZ Tel: 01332 298101 www.bohs.org
Incorporates the Faculty of Occupational Hygiene, which is an examining body in the field of LEV. The Faculty publishes a Directory of Occupational Hygiene Consultants.

British Standards Institution www.bsi-global.com
A leading global provider of management systems assessment and certification solutions.

Chartered Institution of Building Services Engineers (CIBSE), 222 Balham High Road, London SW12 9BS
Tel: 020 8675 5211 www.cibse.org
For engineers designing heating, ventilation and air-conditioning services: professional qualifications.

Chemical Industries Association (CIA), Kings Buildings, Smith Square, London SW1P 3JJ.
Tel: 020 7834 3399 www.cia.org.uk
The UK trade association for the chemical industries.

Confederation of British Industry (CBI) www.cbi.org.uk
Regionally organised, the CBI represents British Industry.

EEF – The Manufacturers' Association, Broadway House, Tothill Street, London SW1H 9NQ
Tel: 020 7222 7777 www.eef.org.uk
Provides a range of health and safety services to members.

Fan Manufacturers' Association (FMA)
www.feta.co.uk/fma
Principles and practice of air extract/supply system design, and offers guidance on fan selection to ensure that such systems perform their intended function efficiently.

The Federation of Environmental Trade Associations (FETA) www.feta.co.uk
The representative body for LEV manufacturers and suppliers.

Heating and Ventilating Contractors' Association (HVCA), Esca House, 34 Palace Court, London W2 4JG
Tel: 020 7313 4900 www.hvca.org.uk
The main representative organisation for companies installing ventilation systems including LEV. Useful publications include DW series.

Independent National Inspection and Testing Association (INITA) www.inita.org.uk
Represents independent companies that conduct inspection and certification of equipment, including LEV systems.

Institution of Occupational Safety and Health (IOSH), The Grange, Highfield Drive, Wigston, Leicestershire LE18 1NN.
Tel: 0116 257 3100 www.iosh.co.uk
Leading body for health and safety professionals. Gives advice on choice of LEV systems.

Safety Assessment Federation (SAFED), Unit 4, First Floor, 70 South Lambeth Road, Vauxhall, London SW8 1RL
Tel: 020 7582 3208 www.safed.co.uk
Represents many insurance companies that conduct inspection and certification of equipment, including LEV systems.

Solids Handling and Processing Association (SHAPA)
www.shapa.co.uk
Represents the major employers in LEV manufacturing.

Trades Union Congress (TUC), Congress House, Great Russell Street, London WC1B 3LS
Tel: 020 7637 4030 www.tuc.org.uk
Gives health and safety advice to members. (See also individual unions, eg AMICUS www.amicustheunion.org.)

UK Accreditation Service (UKAS), 21-47 High Street, Feltham, Middlesex TW13 4UN
Tel: 020 8917 8400 www.ukas.com
Accreditation of various professional activities. UKAS accreditation scheme for 'Thorough examination and test'.

Glossary

Term	Synonyms	Definitions; units	Comments; conversions
ACOP		Approved Code of Practice. This carries greater legal weight in GB courts than 'guidance'.	Check the HSE website for status.
Aerodynamic diameter	Stokes diameter	The diameter of a unit-density sphere that has the same settling velocity in air as the particle in question.	Most workplace sampling is designed to size-select particles on aerodynamic diameter.
Air cleaner	Arrestor	A device to remove contaminants from air, eg filter, cyclone, sock, wet scrubber, electrostatic precipitator (EP).	
Air mover	Fan Propeller fan Axial fan Centrifugal fan Turbo exhauster	Devices that move air.	
Benchmarks		Performance targets, eg flow-rate, pressure, degree of exposure.	
Boundary layer		The stationary or turbulent layers of air near a surface which can hold a contaminant cloud.	
Breathing zone		The region around operators from which they draw air for breathing. Commonly defined as being within 300 mm of nose/mouth.	See publication MDHS14/3[8].
Canopy hood		A receiving hood used over a hot process.	
Capturing hood	Capture hood Captor hood Exterior hood External hood	The source and the contaminant cloud are outside the hood. A capturing hood has to generate sufficient airflow at and around the source to 'capture' and draw the contaminant-laden air into it.	The capturing hood 'reaches out' to capture the contaminant cloud.

Capture velocity		The air velocity, (metres/second) required around a source to capture the contaminant and draw it into the hood.	
Capture zone		A 'three-dimensional envelope' in front of a capturing hood, in which the capture velocity is adequate.	
Clearance time		The time taken for a contaminant to clear from a room or enclosure, once generation has stopped.	
Commissioning	Initial appraisal Intended operating performance Post-installation validation	Proof that an LEV system is capable of providing adequate control.	In the past, adequate commissioning has been rare.
Contaminant cloud		The cloud of contaminated air that disperses from a source.	This may be as a jet, a plume, a puff, or a cloud of vapour evaporating gently.
Cyclone		An air-cleaning device to remove particles from air by centrifugal force.	
Dilution ventilation	General ventilation	A supply of clean air into the workplace, mixing with contaminated air.	Forced dilution uses fans to move air around.
Displacement ventilation	Plug flow Piston flow	Clean air displaces the contaminated air with minimal mixing.	Rarely fully effective due to eddies etc.
Downstream user		Under the REACH Regulation, someone (not the manufacturer or importer) who uses a substance in the course of their industrial or professional activities.	
Duct velocity		The average air velocity measured on a duct cross section (metres/second).	Equals the volume flow rate divided by the cross-sectional area.
Dust cake		The layer of dust that builds up on a fabric filter.	Initially, this improves the filter performance, but airflows reduce and filters can clog.

Dust lamp	Tyndall beam Tyndall lamp	A parallel light beam illuminates the dust cloud to produce forwards light-scattering.	This enables the assessment of particle cloud size and movement.
Duty point		The point of intersection between the fan curve and the system resistance curve.	The duty point must be within the optimum range of the fan.
Eddy		A region in airflow with a rotary motion, contrary to the main flow.	Common with obstructions in airflows and high airflow.
Electrostatic precipitator	EP	A type of particle filter. Charged particles are attracted to a plate of opposite polarity, to which they attach.	
Enclosing hood	Full enclosure Room enclosure Laminar flow rooms Laminar flow booths Enclosing room Clean room Cabin Booth Fume cupboard	A full enclosure contains the process. A room enclosure contains the process and the operator. A partial enclosure contains the process with openings for material and operator access.	Full and room enclosures: the degree of displacement ventilation determines personal exposure and the 'clearance time'.
Face velocity		The average velocity of air at the open front face of a hood or booth (metres/second).	Directly measured or calculated from the volume flow rate divided by the face area.
Fan curve	Fan characteristic curve	Graph of fan pressure, power and efficiency against volume flow rate.	
Flow rates	Linear flow rate Volume flow rate	Units of measurement Linear: metres/second Volume: cubic metres/second	1 m/s = 197 ft/min 1 m^3/s = 2119 cubic ft/min
General ventilation	Ventilation General exhaust ventilation	Air extracted from a space as a whole and replaced.	Can be dilution, displacement or both, and may involve air movers.
Hood		A device to enclose, receive or capture a contaminant cloud.	

Hood face	Hood entrance Hood inlet NOTE: **not** the duct inlet at the back of the hood.	The area at the entrance of a hood; the plane (or planes) between the workplace and the hood interior. For an enclosing hood, the face is all openings that are entry points for workplace air.	The hood face is not always obvious. The face is distinct from slots or filters at the back of a hood ('duct inlet'). While it is useful to measure duct inlet velocity, this must not be confused with face velocity.
Inhalable particles	Total inhalable dust Total dust Inspirable dust	'That fraction of airborne material that enters the nose and mouth and is therefore available for deposition in the respiratory tract.' MDHS 14/3[8]	Includes inspirable, tracheal and respirable dust fractions.
LEV quotation		The LEV that the supplier offers to deliver, including performance and price.	
LEV specification		The employer's (as client) stated requirements for LEV.	See publication INDG408.[2]
Lip extraction	Rim extraction	Extraction slot along one or more sides of an area source such as an open surface tank.	Inappropriate for tanks larger than 1.2 m wide.
Low volume high velocity (LVHV)	On-gun extraction	A method of LEV which uses very small hoods to capture contaminants very close to a source using high-velocity air extraction.	LVHV is usually fitted to hand tools.
Local air displacement (LAD)	Air jet Air blower Air shower/douche Air island	A wide, relatively slow moving jet of air blown into the operator's breathing zone, to displace contaminated air.	See Chapter 7 for details.
Local exhaust ventilation (LEV)	Local extract ventilation Extract ventilation Dust extraction Mist extraction Fume extraction Vapour extraction	The use of extraction to remove contaminated air at or near to its source.	
Make-up air	Replacement air	Air to replace extracted air.	This is part of the LEV system.
Manometer		A simple pressure-indicating device, eg on hoods.	In the past, adequate fitting of manometers has been rare.

Negative pressure		Air pressure lower than that in the workplace.	
Occupational Exposure Limit	OEL	OEL is the usual general acronym.	TLV was the earliest OEL type, and may still be the most widely used type of OELs.
	WEL	Workplace Exposure Limit (GB).	
	MAK	Maximale Arbeitsplatz Konzentration (D).	
	IOELV	Indicative Occupational Exposure Limit Value (EC).	Most OELs refer to 8-hour and 15-minute TWAs.
	DNEL	Derived No Effect Level (EC; REACH).	
	PEL	Permissible Exposure Limits (USA).	
	TLV®	Threshold Limit Values (US ACGIH).	
Piston flow Plug flow	Displacement ventilation	See 'Displacement ventilation'.	
Pitot tube	Pitot-static tube Prandtl tube	A device to measure static and total pressure.	
Plenum		A device to smooth airflows, eg behind the filter in a walk-in booth or in an LAD system.	
Positive pressure		Air pressure higher than that in the workplace.	
Process		The way that airborne contaminants are generated.	Understanding the process means understanding the creation of 'sources'. It can suggest ways to modify the process to reduce the number or size of sources, and contaminant clouds.
Pressure		Units of measurement: Pascals (Pa) Torr = millimetre of mercury (mm Hg) Millibar (mbar) Pound per sq inch (psi) Inch water gauge (WG)	1 mm Hg = 133 Pa 1 mbar = 103 Pa 1 psi = 7237 Pa 1 in WG = 249 Pa
Push-pull	Push-pull hood	An air supply on one side of a contaminant source blows the contaminant cloud towards an extraction hood on the other side.	The hood becomes a receptor.

Qualitative assessment		Assessment by observation.	
Quantitative assessment		Assessment by measurement.	
Receiving hood	Receptor hood Canopy A receiving hood is part of a push-pull system	A receiving hood receives a contaminant cloud, propelled into it with a 'vector' from the process.	Successful receiving hoods intercept contaminant clouds and contain them.
Respirable particles		'The fraction of airborne material that penetrates to the gaseous exchange region of the lung' MDHS14/3[8]	Dust below 10 microns (aerodynamic diameter). Invisible in normal lighting.
Risk management measure	RMM	LEV is a risk management measure under REACH.	Extended Safety Data Sheets for substances and products will stipulate RMMs.
Slot		A long, thin hood with an aspect ratio of 5:1 or greater.	
Source		A process creates a source; the creation of the contaminant cloud.	
Source strength		A combination of the volume rate of release of the contaminant cloud, the cloud volume, shape and speed and the contaminant concentration.	
Static pressure	P_s	Air pressure, measured normal to the flow direction, ie the difference between inside and outside air pressure measured by, eg, a manometer.	
Total pressure		The algebraic sum of the static and velocity pressures.	The pressure exerted by moving air, were it brought to rest.
Time-weighted average	TWA	Airborne contaminant level averaged over a specified period, usually 8 hours or 15 minutes.	The 8-hour TWA is the averaged exposure over 24 hours, adjusted as if it were over 8 hours.
Transport velocity	Conveying velocity	Air velocity to convey particles and prevent deposition in ducts.	

Turbulence		Non-laminar air movement.	
Vapour pressure		The pressure of a vapour in equilibrium with its liquid (or solid) phases.	1 Pa = 9.86 ppm At 25°C, mg/m^3 = ppm x Mol.Wt / 24.45
Velocity pressure	Dynamic pressure (Pv)	Pressure exerted by air due to its motion.	The difference between the total pressure and the static pressure.
Vector	Velocity and direction	The speed and direction of a contaminant cloud.	No/low vector, eg vapour from tank. High vector, eg dust jet from angle grinder.
'Vena contracta'		The section within an opening at which the streamlines first become parallel after entering that opening.	
Wake	Turbulent wake Recirculation zone	A low-pressure region that forms downstream of a body in an airflow.	Complex airflow patterns can appear in the wake downstream of a worker. Contaminant can be drawn into the breathing zone.
Working zone		The volume in the workplace where an activity is generating a contaminant cloud.	